Teaching Literacy Effectively in the Modern Classroom for Ages 5–8

Designed as a "one stop shop" for classroom teachers, this book covers assessment, planning, and progression of writing, spelling, decoding, vocabulary, and comprehension to expand the teaching toolbox.

Dymock and Nicholson explore major focus areas in literacy instruction for teachers based on data-driven research advances. They provide the teacher a handy reference manual to consult when designing lessons to teach young children from diverse backgrounds to help them read and write for success. A general discussion of the research literature is built into the structure of the book to give teachers a knowledge base to teach and explain to children the why and the how of what they are learning. The chapters cover recent concepts of structured literacy, including systematic teaching of decoding skills, vocabulary, comprehension, writing, and spelling. This practical guide uses a scope and sequence approach to teaching that gives children a solid foundation of reading and writing skills. The resources and lesson ideas will engage diverse groups in a classroom, including those at risk of literacy difficulties such as dyslexia, so they also can achieve typical achievement levels for their age – and beyond. Containing a wealth of resources and tips for teaching children ages 5–8, alongside easily downloadable lesson plans, hand-drawn charts, and posters, this book will be of great interest to all classroom teachers involved in teaching literacy.

This resource-filled book will appeal to teachers, professionals, and researchers in teacher training, with a focus on the needs of the teacher, providing practical and insightful ways to teach effectively in diverse classroom settings.

Sue Dymock, originally from Portland, Oregon, started her career as a primary and intermediate school teacher and later became a Senior Lecturer at the University of Waikato (New Zealand) where she taught pre- and in-service teachers for 20 years. Sue's PhD thesis won the National Reading Conference (now Literacy Research Association) outstanding research award; the first time it had been awarded to anyone outside the US. Sue directed the long-running University of Waikato Reading Centre for children with reading difficulties and won a University Community Impact Research Excellence Award for her work. Sue was a Fellow of the International Academy for Research in Learning Disabilities.

Tom Nicholson originally from Sydney, Australia, started his career as a high school teacher, then as a researcher in the Education Department of South Australia. After completing a PhD at the University of Minnesota, he took a University position in New Zealand, taught pre- and in-service teachers for many years, held a personal chair at The University of Auckland, and is currently Professor Emeritus of Education at Massey University. He directed for nearly ten years an after-school literacy programme in inner city Auckland for children. Tom is a member of the Reading Hall of Fame.

Teaching Literacy Effectively in the Modern Classroom for Ages 5–8

A Practical Guide for Teaching Reading and Writing in Diverse Learning Environments

Sue Dymock and Tom Nicholson

Routledge
Taylor & Francis Group

LONDON AND NEW YORK

Designed cover image: Illustrations by Tom Nicholson

First published 2025
by Routledge
4 Park Square, Milton Park, Abingdon, Oxon OX14 4RN

and by Routledge
605 Third Avenue, New York, NY 10158

Routledge is an imprint of the Taylor & Francis Group, an informa business

British Library Cataloguing-in-Publication Data
A catalogue record for this book is available from the British Library

ISBN: 9780367673161 (hbk)
ISBN: 9780367673154 (pbk)
ISBN: 9781003130758 (ebk)

DOI: 10.4324/9781003130758

Typeset in Times New Roman
by KnowledgeWorks Global Ltd.

I'd like to dedicate this book to the memory of the marvellous Dr Sue Dymock, my dear friend and co-writer. We were nearly finished this book when Sue died suddenly. She left a wonderful academic legacy through her research and many publications. Sue directed the successful Children's Reading Centre at Waikato University. Those who knew Sue, like me, will miss her so much.

Contents

Figures and tables

Figures

x *Figures and tables*

Tables

Acknowledgements

Special thanks to Vilija Stephens and to Katie Peace at Routledge for encouraging us to write a book on teaching literacy in the modern classroom. Thanks also to Will Bateman for taking over the proposal while Vilija was on leave. We really went all out to complete the book on time but there were many delays and some personal tragedy when Sue unexpectedly passed away just as we were finishing. We appreciated help and advice in the final stages from Georgia Oman, and Khin Thazin, editorial assistants at Routledge. A final thanks to our families for their unswerving support.

Copyright permissions

Thanks to Dame Wendy Pye for allowing us to reprint the text of *Andrew and Sue make a kite*. It is from the Sunshine Phonics Decodables series.

Thanks to Professor James Chapman for permission to use the Invented Spelling Test.

Thanks to Emeritus Professor Philip Gough for permission to use the GKR Phonemic Awareness Test.

About the authors

Sue Dymock unexpectedly passed away in November 2023. She was a Senior Lecturer in Education at the University of Waikato. Tom Nicholson is Professor Emeritus at Massey University. The authors started their careers in classroom teaching. They worked in university settings for many years, especially in teacher training programmes.

Preface to the book

Aims and scope

Aims

The major aim of the book is to be a handy reference manual, a "one stop shop" for teachers. It is a result of countless hours of reading the research, looking for practical and proven ways to teach effectively. The book is not without theory and research but the focus is on the practical needs of the teacher. It is a book for the classroom.

Scope

It is for the "modern classroom" which means not just a classroom with internet and digital technology but a classroom that is diverse, likely to include students from second language backgrounds, poverty backgrounds, or with difficulties requiring the teacher to dig deep into their teaching toolbox – e.g., dyslexia, ADHD, etc. The book explains how to teach the foundation skills, that is, decoding and spelling. It also goes beyond these foundations to cover the higher level skills required to read and write well. This is the modern classroom.

Who this book is for

When we wrote this book, we were thinking of three different kinds of teachers. There was the new graduate, fresh out of training. There was the experienced teacher starting the challenge of a new class at a different level. Finally, the teacher who was looking for some new insights, a go-to resource.

The newbie teacher

You are new to teaching, finished your degree. You are thinking "what now." Your mind is full of theory but what you want is a compass, a guide that translates theory into actions you can use in the classroom, not just fluffy activities but ones that really work. This book delivers the practice you need to teach effectively.

The teacher facing a new challenge

You are an experienced teacher but your assignment this year is to teach a different year level. It is unfamiliar territory, full of unknowns. This book will guide you through uncharted waters, especially if you have struggling students with specific needs.

The curious teacher

The experienced, seasoned teacher who is looking for that one-stop shop that fills in the gaps in traditional university training. This is the book you need. It shows, step-by-step, what theory looks like in practice. It is practical without overwhelming with detail.

This book will be your trusted guide to teaching children aged 5–8 to read and write successfully.

Part I
Decoding Skills

1 Decoding

What is it?

1.1 Introduction

Learning to decode seems easy enough to the adult who can read, but it is not easy for the beginner. Ahead of them are three major "speed bumps." First, the graphemes, the letters of the alphabet. They are hard to learn and are abstract squiggles. Second, the phonemes, the spoken alphabet of speech; phonemic awareness is not something that young children learn naturally. Third, it is difficult to discover the letter-sound rules of English writing, the rules are not intuitively obvious for many children, and beginner readers will need the teacher to help them learn the rules.

The English language and its writing system has undergone much change over many hundreds of years. The novice reader is digging into an archaeological site with a long history and several different spelling systems that have come about through waves of invasions by foreign powers, including the Romans, the Anglo-Saxons, and the Normans from France. The scientific revolution in the 1500s brought many thousands of words into the language from Latin and Greek. English is a melting pot of words from different languages. Children need to know all this, it demystifies English, and it explains the exciting nature of English spelling. It is the "Story of English."

This chapter will cover the following topics:

- What is decoding skill?
- Teaching decoding – how to avoid speed bumps
- Phonemic awareness – why children need it
- The Story of English writing – the big picture
- Cracking the "cipher" of Anglo-Saxon writing
- Why some children learn to read words while others fail

1.2 Decoding and "the simple view" of reading

A definition of decoding is the ability to map the letters (or graphemes) in written words to a storage place or "letter box" in the brain that is our mental dictionary of words, and in that letter box, we store the meanings of words, their sounds (or phonemes), and their printed forms (the orthographic forms – the correct spellings).

DOI: 10.4324/9781003130758-2

This seems fine, but how does decoding fit into the bigger scheme of things? What has it got to do with real reading?

It is easy to think of decoding as a minor skill, as a not very important part of real reading, but in fact it is essential for reading. It is part of the science of reading and how children learn to read.

A widely regarded model of reading acquisition is the *Simple View of Reading* (SVR) (Gough & Tunmer, 1986; Hoover & Gough, 1990; Hoover & Tunmer, 2020, 2022). The model says that reading (R) is a result of the interaction of decoding skill (D) and language comprehension (LC). The relationship between decoding and language is expressed in multiplicative form, that $R = D \times LC$. The formula looks complex, but it is quite straightforward in what it says about reading.

To learn to read well, children need decoding expertise and language knowledge. If one or both factors are weak, they will not learn to read. It predicts that reading difficulty can be a result of weakness in either decoding or language or both.

On one side of the coin, if the child lacks the ability to decode words (i.e., $D = 0$), then even if their language knowledge is perfect (LC $=1$), they will not be able to read ($0 \times 1 = 0$).

What is an example of a situation where $D = 0$? Well, it describes almost every school beginner. Young children, when they first start school, generally have a surprisingly good ability to speak and comprehend English, given their young age (Gough & Hillinger, 1980). In other words, they have a high level of LC; it is something they learn naturally as they grow up – but almost all of them have little or no decoding skill or D, they mostly cannot read a word ($D = 0$).

On the other side of the coin, the SVR says that if the child has perfect decoding ($D = 1$) but cannot understand oral language (LC $= 0$), then they will still not be able to read ($1 \times 0 = 0$).

What is an example of LC $= 0$? Well, this might be the situation for an immigrant child who has come from, say Italy, they may already know how to decode words in Italian because they learned to do that in school in their own country, but if they cannot understand the English language, they will not be able to understand what they read in English. In addition, a low level of LC might also be the case for a child with a specific language impairment. There may be other factors as well that account for a lower level of LC.

To learn to read children need both decoding skill or D and language comprehension ability or LC. They are both important. The beginner reader needs both. Decoding is not enough on its own to learn to read, and language is not enough on its own, but together the child will read. In the SVR model, the Reader is someone with a high level of D and LC. To read with comprehension, the child must be able to decode the written text and understand the language it is written in.

The SVR model helps to explain a classroom situation where the teacher finds some children can decode their beginner reading books perfectly but do not understand what they read. This is because they do not understand the language of the text. One study found this was the reason for their difficulty because they did not understand even when the text was read aloud to them (Dymock, 1993). The problem was not decoding (D) but language (LC). As the SVR model says, to read well, you need both skills.

The SVR also helps to explain a classroom situation where children have excellent language skills but cannot decode the words on the page. This is the case with dyslexia, where children often have very high oral language scores on tests but experience severe difficulties in learning to decode words (Nicholson & Dymock, 2023). This is exactly what the SVR model predicts, that it is not enough to have a high level of LC, the child needs a high level of D as well.

The good news for teachers is that the vast majority of English-speaking children, when they start school, already have a high level of English language skill. Teachers do not have to teach them to talk. As part of their evolutionary inheritance, in most cases, children in every country, every language, and every household learn to talk simply by exposure to the language spoken around them. They are not blank slates when they enter the classroom. Their language is not as advanced as for adults, and it does not have the same depth of grammar, vocabulary, and general knowledge, but it is surprisingly skilful (Harley, 2017). What school beginners' lack, however, is the ability to decode. Almost invariably, the school beginner is unable to read a word. This is the main task for the teacher in the first years of school, to teach them how to unlock the spellings of words.

1.3 Teaching decoding – what can go wrong – how to fix it

We must teach decoding, that is, the letter-sound rules of English writing. It seems simple enough. Can anything possibly go wrong? Nothing can go wrong, but sometimes when the teacher steps back from the hurly-burly of a busy classroom, and takes a closer look, they see that some children are not learning. Consider these two scenarios that show how sometimes the best laid lessons can go astray.

Scenario 1 – Learning the alphabet. Each day, first thing in the morning, these beginner readers chant together the ABC – "ay, ah, apple, bee, beh, butterfly, cee, keh, cat, dee, deh, dog, ee, eh, elephant" – and so on. There is a chorus of letters and words, and the atmosphere is loud and lively. You watch the class, but as you watch closely, you notice that while some confidently lead the way, others stumble, and some are silent. Is the task cognitively too complex? For some, yes it is. These beginners are having to learn four different things at once, the alphabet names, their sounds, the upper case forms of letters, and the lowercase forms as well.

Clearly, for some of the class, the cognitive load is too much. Some were lost or confused. So the question is, why teach the alphabet this way? Why not teach just one thing at a time? A simple change like teaching just the *sounds* of the letters and just the lowercase forms would make the task much more achievable for every student.

Scenario 2 – Now imagine a Year 1 class where the class looks forward to reading a new decodable book, but before doing so the publisher's teacher handbook requires that children need to read correctly a list of 30 isolated words at the front of the book. The time one child takes to read the words, some 15 minutes, raises the question of whether this is the most practical way for children to practise their decoding skills. What message are we sending to these beginners?

Decodable books certainly can help children put their phonics knowledge into practice but having to face a list of 30 words that are hard to decode seems to be sending some students the message that they are failures. This is where the teacher has to consider a change of tack. If the list of words is too difficult, then surely the decodable book is too difficult. Should the teacher select a decodable book that fits better with the class' current decoding skills or perhaps try a different approach like reading the book first and then after reading the book, review the list of words with the class.

To the outside observer, in cases like this, the designers of early literacy programmes are not taking into account that the task is too hard. They are expecting children to run before they can walk. We create complexity, unwittingly, when simplicity is much more effective.

The message of these two different scenarios is that sometimes the school reading programme can leave children lost at sea while the ship sails on. We make it too hard to work out the letter-sound rules of English writing. If we see that some children are not learning, it is a signal to slow the ship down and simplify the task, to restructure the lessons.

On the one hand, these scenarios and the problems they describe can make the task of teaching decoding feel overwhelming. On the other hand, it is actually a good thing; it shows that teaching is not about blindly following the programme given. In the above scenarios, the knowledgeable teacher can see children are struggling and will think outside the square to solve the issues. Sometimes, slowing down, keeping it simple, and using a step-by-step teaching approach, slow and steady, will make a huge positive difference to their progress.

1.4   Phonemic awareness – an essential prerequisite to decoding

One roadblock in learning to decode words is a lack of phonemic awareness. If the child lacks this awareness, they will struggle to decode. If they do not know, for example, that the first sound in *sun* is /s/, it will be hard for them to understand what the teacher means when they say that the letter *s* has the /s/ sound.

There is much evidence to show that phonemic awareness helps learning to decode words. First, phonemic awareness predicts decoding progress. If you have phonemic awareness, it is easier to learn to read. Second, most children with severe reading difficulties lack phonemic awareness. It will be hard for them to read the word *dog* if they are unaware that /dog/ has three sounds (i.e., phonemes), /d-o-g/. Third, studies have found that if we teach phonemic awareness then it helps children with decoding words. This is especially the case if we teach phonemic awareness at the same time as teaching the 26 alphabet letters (Castle et al., 1994; Ehri et al., 2001; Gough & Lee, 2007; Johnston & Watson, 2004; Rehfeld et al., 2022; Rice et al., 2022).

Writing, very simply, is speech written down. In English, speech is written as a series of letter-sounds. We write *dog* as *d-o-g*. It seems obvious to an adult who can decode but many young children when they start school do not understand this. They may think that /sandwich/ starts with /san/ and that /biscuit/ starts with /bis/. They will not know the first sound in their name. They know that words mean something, but they do not know that words are made of phonemes, e.g., we asked some five-year-old children questions such as, "What are the two sounds in /no/?" One child said, "No thank you." We asked, "What are the two sounds in /up/? Another said, "Go up." We asked, "What word is /n-i-ce/?" Another said, "You're nice."

What exactly is phonemic awareness? It is part of a more general awareness of speech, called phonological awareness – as shown in Figure 1.1. This is knowledge of the structure of words at a wider level. It is knowing that /rabbit/ is a word. In addition it is knowing that /rabbit/ has two syllables, /rab-bit/. A syllable is "a unit of speech containing a vowel and any consonants preceding or following that vowel" (Henry, 2010, p. 314).

It is also knowing that a syllable can break into parts – onset and rime. The consonants before the vowel make up the "onset" of the syllable. The vowel and the consonants that follow it (if any) within the syllable make up the "rime." This is the "onset-rime" structure. So we can break the first syllable /rab/ in /rabbit/ into its onset /r/ and rime /ab/, and we can break the second syllable /bit/, into /b/ and /it/.

We can then break the onset and the rime into phonemes, /r-a-b/ and /b-i-t/. A phoneme is "the smallest unit of sound that conveys a distinction in meaning" (Henry, 2010, p. 312).

A student who has phonemic awareness has "the insight that spoken words are made up of a sequence of separable sounds" (Graves et al., 2004, p. 93) and "the ability to manipulate sounds in words" (Henry, 2010, p. 312).

In the English language, there are 44 phonemes, with slight variance depending on dialect. The 26 letters of the alphabet represent these 44 phonemes. Since there are more phonemes than letters, each phoneme can be represented by a single letter, e.g., *b*, or by a combination of letters, e.g., *ch, ow*.

Levels of Phonological Awareness: Word, Syllable, Onset-rime, Phoneme

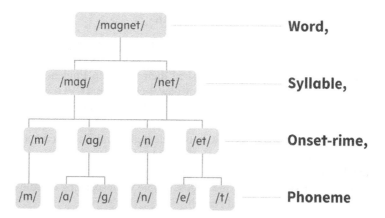

Figure 1.1 Levels of Phonological Awareness – Word, Syllable, Onset-rime, and Phoneme

Teaching phonemic awareness to young children does not need to take much class time during the school year. Ehri et al. (2001) suggested between 5 and 18 hours total and no more. Unwittingly, some programmes go way beyond this suggested time, e.g., 30–40 hours (Brown et al., 2021). What should a teacher do? The important thing to check is that the class has this awareness when they are learning to read. If they have it, then you have done your job, no need to continue teaching it.

1.5   The Story of English

English writing has a long history (Calfee, 1984; Nist, 1966). First, the Roman conquest of England in 50 AD brought the 24 letters of the Roman alphabet to England. This arrival of the alphabet enabled scribes in later years to write down the language of the people.

At the time of the Romans, and after they withdrew their troops from England, there was no common "English" language. This started to change with the invasions of the Angles and Saxons, in the years 700–800. As these tribes dominated, their Anglo-Saxon language became the norm that we now call Old English.

The next important step in the Story of English was the Norman invasion of England in 1066. Their rule lasted 300 years and introduced many French words. The scientific revolution in the 1500s brought many more loan words to the language from Greek and Latin to describe new discoveries.

All these layers of language, as well as many other borrowed words from probably 100 or more languages, have brought about modern English. The main layers of English vocabulary have their origins in Anglo-Saxon, Latin/French, and Greek words. There are different decoding rules for each layer. Children need to learn these. At the start, though, the focus of teaching is on the first layer of words, the Anglo-Saxon layer that we know as Old English. These are the everyday words of English. The Old English layer is rich with Anglo-Saxon words. Did you know that more than 90% of words in Shakespeare's plays are from the Anglo-Saxon layer?

1.6   The Anglo-Saxon layer of English

At the beginning of the Current Era (AD 0), England was populated by Celts (Britons and Irish), followed by Romans, and then in the middle of the first millennium Anglo-Saxon warriors smashed their way into England. The Anglo-Saxon language had a basically consonant-vowel-consonant (CVC) structure, with many three- and four-letter words, and compound words (Calfee, 2005).

Other invaders were the Jutes and the Vikings. The Vikings nearly took over the whole country but King Alfred made peace and also encouraged books to be written in the language of the people, Old English. With the French invasion more and longer words came into the English language. Many Latin words came with the arrival of missionaries. By the 1400s, people were speaking Middle English, a mix of Anglo-Saxon, Latin, and French.

In 1476 Caxton introduced the printing press to England. They printed anything written in English, e.g., Chaucer's *Canterbury Tales*. In the 1500s, many more complex words came into the language. It was the age of Science, e.g., Newton and Bacon. It was the age of literature, e.g., Shakespeare. This became the modern English we speak and write today.

The beginner reader of English has to start with Anglo-Saxon words. These are the everyday words of English, the words most children speak and understand when they start school.

Table 1.1 shows the main Anglo-Saxon decoding patterns (Calfee & Associates, 1981; Calfee & Patrick, 1995). The first thing to notice in Table 1.1 is the structure. It is not a random list of rules to teach. It has a logical structure. The upper half of the table contains the consonant sounds. The consonants are either singletons (on their own), clusters (two to three consonants), or digraphs (two consonants, usually making a new sound).

The lower half of the table contains the vowel sounds. There are single vowels (short vowel sounds), single vowels + final e to make the long vowel sound, vowels affected by r- and l-, and vowel digraphs (two vowels together) that also represent long vowel sounds. The teacher needs to teach these patterns, using a logical scope and sequence of instruction, from consonant-short vowel-consonant (CVC) patterns upward.

Many Anglo-Saxon words are made of consonant and vowel combinations as shown in Table 1.1 (Calfee & Associates, 1981). The words are short, either one or two syllables in length.

Another key aspect of the Anglo-Saxon writing system is that it is morphophonemic (Calfee, 2005). The morphophonemic principle says that when decoding a word we should first look to see if we can divide it into its component morphemes, e.g., many Anglo-Saxon words are compounds of two separate words, e.g., *with-hold*. It is so important with this word to use the morphophonemic principle to see that it is two words combined and that the "th" is one sound /th/. Otherwise, the child may incorrectly think it is *wit-hhold*.

The morphophonemic principle is also evident in the many Anglo-Saxon words that use suffixes such as -s(es), -ed, -ing, -er, -ly to create derivatives of base words, e.g., *peach-peaches*, *pit-pitted*, *sad-sadder*, and *slow-slowly*.

As shown in Table 1.1, the single consonants mostly represent one phoneme (but *c, g, s, y* can vary). The consonant blends (or clusters) are double or triple consonant sounds, they occur at the beginning or end of the word – but they are not new sounds to learn. The consonant digraphs are mostly new sounds. The ancient scribes invented most of these spellings by adding an h to existing letters to form ch, sh, th, and wh. The good news is there are not many of these digraphs.

The vowels are more complex. If a single vowel or vowel combination is between two consonants, its phoneme sound is either short or long. This is a key thing for children to learn; the vowels have two sounds, short and long. Caxton, who brought the printing press to England, is thought to be the person who introduced the final e rule to mark the short and long single vowel sound (Calfee, 2005). Caxton's printers added a final e to the end of the word to signal that the preceding vowel sound had a long sound. This became known as the final e or "silent e" rule. The final e was also used as a marker for to solve other problems, e.g., printers did not like words to end in *v*, so they added a final e – e.g., *have, love,* and *give.*

To keep the short vowel sound, another marking rule was to double the consonant after the first vowel, e.g., diner-dinner, later-latter to indicate the short vowel sound. This was the "doubling rule", sometimes called the "rabbit rule."

Then there are r- and l-affected vowel sounds. When a short vowel is followed by an *r*, the *r* affects the sound of the vowel, e.g., *ar, or, er, ir,* and *ur*. For example, *bid/ bird, had/hard*. This especially applies to the short vowel *a* followed by *l* because it changes its sound to /or/ (e.g., *talk*). In Table 1.1, there is a column for r- and l-affected vowels. The /r/ and /l/ are consonant sounds but they also act as semi-vowels.

Some vowel digraphs, e.g., *ee, ai, oa, au,* and *aw* are consistent in sound, i.e., represent one sound (or phoneme). They are one-sound vowel digraphs.

Other vowel digraphs represent two sounds. The two sound digraphs have two different sounds, e.g., *ea – bread, leaf, ow – cow, tow*.

When teaching the two-sound digraphs, a good idea is to keep practising until students are fluent with one-sound digraphs. Then teach the two sound vowel digraphs. The two-sound vowel digraphs are harder to remember and will require more practice. Reading of decodable books that have two-sound digraph patterns will help because in the context of the story it will be clear to the child which of the two sounds to use, e.g., the OO in *the moon shines on the roof*.

Table 1.1 Anglo-Saxon Spelling Patterns.

Consonants

Single	Clusters	Digraphs
s t p n m d g c k r h b f l j v w x y z q	Initial bl br cl cr dr fl fr gl gr pl pr sc sk sm sl sn sp st sw tr tw scr spl spr squ str shr thr Final - ft -mp -nt -lk	Initial ch sh th wh Final -ng

Vowels

Single Short – Long	r- and l-controlled	Digraphs
a: mad made e: pet Pete i: bit bite o: hop hope u: cut cute	ar: park or: corn er: fern ir: bird ur: surf al: call, walk	one sound: ai/ay pain, play ee meet igh night oa boat ue/ew blue, screw au/aw haunt, saw oi/oy oil, toy two sounds: ea leaf, bread oo moon, cook ou house soup ow cow tow ie pie, thief ei weight, protein

1.7   Research on the best way to teach decoding

The "science" of reading supports a structured approach to teaching decoding. Meta-analysis research, where the results of many studies are averaged to find a general pattern of effectiveness, has found that on average, when you look at the effects of a large number of studies, that systematic and structured teaching of decoding, especially using phonics, is more effective than other approaches (e.g., Galuschka et al., 2020; National Reading Panel [NICHD], 2000; Suggate, 2016).

An influential example of the success of structured teaching using a decoding approach was a study in Clackmannanshire in Scotland (Johnston & Watson, 2005) that taught phonics to a large group of five-year-olds. The study found that after 10 weeks of structured, synthetic phonics, the group who received this instruction were reading ahead of their chronological age, compared with a control group who did not get this teaching. When re-assessed at age 12, the phonics children were still reading words well ahead of their chronological age and comprehending what they read.

One feature of the study was that teachers taught the 26 letter-sounds more quickly than the control group. The phonics children learned one letter-sound a day while the control group learned one letter-sound a week. This speed in learning may have propelled the phonics children forward. The results of that study influenced a change of policy in England (Rose, 2006) toward teaching synthetic phonics and led to the implementation of a new reading curriculum called *Letters and Sounds* (Department for Education and Skills, 2007).

1.8   Why some children learn to read while others fail

Despite years of academic training, many preservice teachers feel unprepared to teach decoding skills to children, especially phonics (Meeks & Kemp, 2017), possibly because lectures discussing essential decoding skills get very little academic coverage (Meeks & Stephenson, 2020). Students learn in their training they need to teach decoding but they may not learn how to teach these essential decoding skills. Such phonological knowledge seems to help teacher self-belief and self-agency for teaching of decoding skills (Nicholson & McIntosh, 2020).

Without decoding skill, many children will fail to read. There are other options to read words besides decoding, but these options will not end well. One option for the beginner is to memorise words by their look, but this is not a good way to go; there are too many words to memorise; they can perhaps memorise 30 or 40 words, but soon too many words will look the same (Gough & Hillinger, 1980). This may be why many beginners confuse words like dad/sad, I/is, we/went, and dog/girl – all these words have some visual similarity.

Another option is to use context clues and pictures in text reading to work out words, but this seems also the wrong way to go: "Context can help, and surely does, sometimes. Yet context is a false friend. Context helps the child with predictable words, but less – if at all – with unpredictable words ...

Context helps the child where she needs it least, and lets her down where she needs it most" (Gough, 1993, p. 88).

Context clues have only limited predictive power in terms of decoding words. Context can help with function words like "the" but not with content words that carry the main meaning of the text (Gough, 1983, 1996; Nicholson & Hill, 1985). Sophisticated guessing of words is not what skilled readers do. Skilled readers do not need to guess. They simply decode the words. Only beginners and older, unskilled readers have to rely on context to guess words (Castles et al., 2018; Nicholson, 1991; Nicholson & Tunmer, 2010). To teach children to guess words with context clues rather than sound them out may work for some but for many children it will not end well.

The aim of this and the next chapters is to give the teacher effective methods to teach decoding, ones that will work, that will enable all children to decode words with success.

1.9   Conclusion

Well, that was a quick introduction to decoding – what it is. Decoding skill is essential for reading success. Students need systematic instruction to learn the skills. They need to follow a structured approach with a clear scope and sequence – as described in the next chapters.

Success in reading in the early grades is all about learning the morphophonemic nature of the Anglo-Saxon writing system, that words follow certain morphemic and letter-sound rules. It is so worth spending time teaching children to decode words well. You are teaching a critical skill for learning to read.

2　Assessing decoding

2.1　Introduction

Teachers have good intuitions about children's decoding levels, but sometimes it is hard to explain why students are at that level, or what to do about it. It is one thing to diagnose a problem, another to resolve it. Assessment helps teachers to understand where children are at in their decoding skills. Using formal and informal measures is like bringing in an outside expert to see what is happening. It is more objective. It gives insights as to what action to take.

Intuitions are valuable. There are many times when the teacher has to act intuitively, to make quick decisions. On the other hand, backing up intuitions with objective data is important.

Sometimes students seem to be doing fine, but they unwittingly mask their difficulties, and we do not see that they are struggling to learn. It is not clear why they do this, perhaps they want to please the teacher and not seem "dumb," yet they are in fact way behind their classmates. The teacher thinks they are progressing, but they are not. Informal observations in classroom can give insights as to where they are struggling and why. Only by assessing children's progress can the teacher gain a more complete picture as to the why and what of their decoding journey.

This chapter will cover the following topics:

- Standardised assessments
- Informal assessment – alphabet knowledge
- Informal assessment – phonemic awareness
- Informal assessment – basic decoding skills
- A case study assessment example

2.2　Standardised assessments

There are a number of standardised measures of real and non-word reading available on the internet and from publishers. A stumbling block for teachers is that very often the published measures are not accessible in the classroom because specialist training in assessment is required for purchase.

DOI: 10.4324/9781003130758-3

So how do we assess decoding skills? In order to assess non-word decoding skills, this chapter includes an informal measure of decoding skill, the *Alien Words Test* – see Table 2.3.

In addition, however, the teacher should use standardised tests of word reading. They are normed on a wider population, and they do indirectly have diagnostic value in that unless children have some decoding skills, they will not be able to read the list of graded words in the test.

Standardised tests give an indication of how a child decodes words compared with other children of the same age. It is important for the teacher to know whether their students are able to decode words as well as their peers.

We have used two-word reading measures that do not require the teacher to have specialist training. The Schonell Word Reading Test (Schonell & Schonell, 1956) gives a word reading age. Here is an internet link – https://assessment.tki.org.nz/media/files/QRS-files/SchonellReading. The Burt Word Reading Test (see Nicholson, 2005; Nicholson & Dymock, 2023) also does not require specialist training and gives a word reading age.

2.3   Informal assessments

Assessment 1 – Alphabet knowledge

Children cannot begin to decode words properly unless they can quickly and accurately identify the 26 letter-sounds of the alphabet. Assessing their alphabet knowledge involves checking ability to identify all the names and sounds of the 26 letters of the alphabet. Some children when they start school will know all or most of the names and sounds of the alphabet, but many may know only some of the letter-sounds and some may not know any sounds.

Even older children can vary in speed and accuracy of their alphabet knowledge. It is helpful to check. Table 2.1 is a copy of a test that the teacher can use. The test has 26 uppercase and 26 lowercase letters all in random order. Ask the student to say the names of the letters. Then ask them to say the sounds of the letters. Note for teacher – score with blue pen for sounds and red pen for names. Score out of 26 for upper and lower case names and sounds. If an error, write it down.

Table 2.1 Alphabet Test.

r	o	n	l	m	
y	t	v	k	p	
z	i	a	j	u	
s	h	b	c	g	
w	d	f	x	q	e
B	A	I	S	C	
D	F	E	P	T	
L	M	R	Z	J	
U	H	G	W	X	
Q	K	V	Y	N	O

Assessment 2 – Phonemic awareness

It is important to assess phonemic awareness. Some children have difficulty with learning to decode words because they lack phonemic awareness. The teacher needs to identify children who need some help to build their awareness.

Phonemic awareness is the ability to deconstruct spoken words into their component sounds. Some children starting school will have an awareness of phonemes in words, e.g., they can segment /up/ into its sounds /u-p/, but some will lack this awareness. One school beginner we tested said that the two sounds in /up/ were /up/ and /down/.

An informal measure we have used extensively is the *GKR Phonemic Awareness Test*. There are six subtests in the *GKR*, each with seven items. An average benchmark score to aim for would be a score of 30 out of 42 at the end of the first year of school and 36 out of 42 at the end of the second year of school (Juel et al., 1986). If children in the class score significantly below 30, the teacher should consider adding phonemic awareness activities to their lessons.

Table 2.2 shows the six subtests of the full version of the *GKR Phonemic Awareness Test*. The GKR assesses a range of phonemic skills (blending, segmenting, deletion, and substitution). It has good reliabilities (Juel et al., 1986; Tse & Nicholson, 2014). The teacher reads the test items aloud and scores the responses. The student does not see the test. Critical subtests to check for beginning reading are subtest 1 blending and subtest 4 segmenting. These basics are essential starting points (Gough & Lee, 2007).

Examples of the items in each subtest are below:

1 Blending – the first item is /nice/. The teacher says to the child, e.g., "Say/ n-i-ce/, what word is/n-i-ce/." The teacher has to stretch out the phonemes and avoid giving a schwa sound, e.g., do not say neh-ie-seh. Try to stretch the word like a rubber band, say slowly, /n-i-ce/.

Table 2.2 GKR Phonemic Awareness Test – Teacher Copy.

Notes for the teacher: Keep in mind that this is not for the student to read. You have to read out the questions to them. Give the practice item first in each subtest. Explain the practice item if the child seems confused. Be sure to encourage the student after each item, "That's good, OK, let's try another one." The answers to each item are in parentheses in the test form below, but do not tell the child any of the answers – they are just for you – for scoring. Total of 42 items. Approximate benchmarks in terms of expected scores at the end of the first year of school would be 30 out of 42 correct and at the end of the second year of school, 36 out of 42.

1. Blending
Practice: Say s-u-n. What word is s-u-n?
  (answer = sun)

n-i-ce	(nice)
t-oo	(too)
h-e	(he)
r-a-ke	(rake)
t-r-ai-n	(train)
p-l-a-ne	(plane)
f-u-nn-y	(funny)

2. Deletion of first phoneme
Practice: Say sun. Say sun without the s
  (Answer = un)

top (t)	(op)
gasp (g)	(asp)
find (f)	(ind)
paint (p)	(aint)
up (u)	(p)
at (a)	(t)
so (s)	(o)

(Continued)

Table 2.2 (Continued)

3. Deletion of last phoneme		4. Phonemic segmentation	
Practice: Say sun. Say sun without the n. (Answer = su)		Practice: Say sun. What are the (3) phonemes in sun? (Answer = s-u-n)	
same (m)	(say)	2 no	(n-o)
me (e)	(m)	2 at	(a-t)
ate (t)	(ay)	2 up	(u-p)
go (o)	(g)	3 keep	(k-ee-p)
frog (g)	(fro)	3 man	(m-a-n)
grab (b)	(gra)	3 teeth	(t-ee-th)
stride (d)	(stri)	4 into	(i-n-t-o)

5. Substitution of first phoneme				6. Substitution of final phoneme			
Practice: Say sun. Now, instead of /s/ start the new word with /f/. (Answer = fun)				Practice: Say sun. Now, instead of /n/ end the new word with /p/. (Answer = sup)			
ball	b	c	(call)	park	k	t	(part)
goat	g	b	(boat)	run	n	g	(rug)
took	t	c	(cook)	late	t	m	(lame)
fish	f	d	(dish)	mess	s	n	(men)
two	t	z	(zoo)	rope	p	d	(rode)
chair	ch	p	(pair)	fame	m	s	(face)
meat	m	f	(feet)	wet	t	b	(web)
Total Score = ____/42							

Source: © Gough-Kastler-Roper Phonemic Awareness Test, reprinted with permission of Professor Emeritus Philip Gough (see also Roper, 1984).

2 Delete first phoneme – the first item is /top/. The teacher says to the child, "Say/top/. Now say /top/ without the /t/." The student mentally has to delete the first sound /t/ and say what remains, which is /op/.

3 Delete last phoneme – one of the items is /same/. The teacher says to the child, "Say /same/. Now say /same/ without the /m/." The student mentally has to delete the last sound /m/ and say what remains, which is /say/.

4 Segmenting – the first item is /no/. The teacher says to the child, "Say/no/. Now say the two sounds in/no/." Student has to segment the two sounds and say /n-o/. Encourage them not to spell out the word using letter names like "en-oh" or letter sounds "neh-oh."

5 Substitute first phoneme – the first item is /ball/. The teacher says to the child, "Say /ball/. Now, instead of /b/, start the new word with /c/." This task requires the student to delete mentally the initial phoneme /b/ and then substitute another phoneme /c/. The student has to say /call/.

6 Substitute last phoneme – the first item is /park/. The teacher says, "Say /park/. Now, instead of /k/, end the new word with /t/." This task requires the student to delete the final phoneme /k/ and replace it with another phoneme /t/. The student has to say /part/.

Assessment 3 – Basic decoding skills – "Alien Words" Test

A non-word reading measure is a "pure" measure of decoding skill. When teaching beginners, it provides the teacher with information about emerging decoding skill. It involves the student in decoding a list of non-words. This type of measure has more diagnostic value than a test of reading real words because it controls for the effects of prior knowledge and "sight words," i.e., words memorised visually. The only way the child can "read" these non-words they have never seen before is to decode them phoneme by phoneme.

The *Alien Words Test* in Table 2.3 consists of 50 non-words, adapted from the *Bryant Test of Basic Decoding Skills* (Bryant, 1975). To administer the test, make a copy of the test for yourself and the student. Before they start, remind them that these are alien words. They are not real words. Ask the pupil to read the words starting from the first column, reading down the column. Put a check ✓ next to the correct word, and if an error, write down the response. Stop after ten consecutive errors if the student is having serious difficulty. Try not to let the student see your scoring of the test.

A benchmark score for a student would be 20 out of 50 correct after a year of school and 30 out of 50 correct after two years of school (Juel et al., 1986).

An option to consider if the teacher for some reason does not have time to assess each child in the class individually is to give the Alien Words test as a spelling test. This way, the teacher can give the test to the whole class in one sitting. It is not the same as a reading test but it will give a general indication of the decoding skills of the class as a whole. Skilled readers are usually skilled spellers, and vice versa. You will need to be flexible in marking, e.g., the test word "fene" could be spelled several ways as *fene, fean,* and *feen*.

Table 2.3 Alien Words Test.

Student name _____
Date _____
Age _____

1	gub	21	fene	41	bafnov
2	sot	22	yate	42	rulnupe
3	tid	23	bome	43	defov
4	vef	24	nupe	44	giction
5	cag	25	kibe	45	prefene
6	puv	26	phune	46	uncubeness
7	hod	27	che	47	exyated
8	bik	28	sho	48	senwoxable
9	kel	29	whu	49	befkubber
10	zam	30	thide	50	vamozful
11	jun	31	smaw		
12	fep	32	frew		
13	quib	33	gler		
14	rog	34	slar		
15	naz	35	twor		
16	lut	36	treef		
17	mav	37	cloob		
18	yox	38	prail		
19	weg	39	broy		
20	diz	40	droaf		

Analysing the scores

Items 1–20 check the three-letter consonant-vowel-consonant (CVC) pattern. If the students can decode these CVC non-word patterns, they have basic skills to read words like *sat*, *dog*, *web*, and *zip*.

Items 21–25 check the split digraph rule. If the students can decode these "silent e" words, they have the skills to decode real words with the split vowel digraph (final e) pattern like *cake* and *bone*.

Items 26–30 check consonant digraphs. If the students can decode these digraph words, they have the skills to decode real words like *chick*, *shop*, *them*, and *fish*.

Items 31–40 give information on two decoding skills: (1) consonant clusters – the words all start with clusters, and (2) long vowel sounds, including r-affected

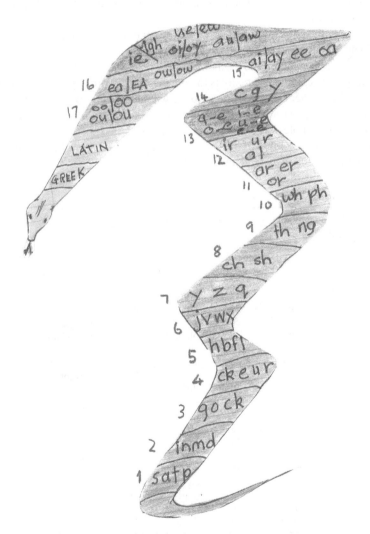

Figure 2.1 Step-by-step Scope and Sequence for Decoding Instruction in the Early Years

vowels and vowel digraphs. If the students can decode these non-words, they have the basic skills to decode real words with different consonant clusters. They also will be able to decode words with r-affected vowels (e.g., *start* and *storm*) and different vowel digraphs (e.g., *crook, broom, Troy, mail, sleep, coat, straw,* and *stew*).

Items 41–50 are two-syllable and Latin-based words. If the students can decode these non-word patterns, they have the basic skills to decode real multi-syllable words like *napkin, magnet,* and *trombone* and Latin-based words, like *transportable* and *destruction*.

To decide what action to take based on *Alien Words Test* scores, use the scope and sequence diagram in Figure 2.1 as a guide to what letter-sounds to focus on. Steps 1–7 cover CVC words, steps 8–10 cover consonant digraphs, steps 11–12 cover r- and l-controlled vowels, step 13 covers split vowel digraphs, step 14 covers chameleon letters c, g, y, and steps 15–17 cover one- and two-sound vowel digraphs. To teach multi-syllable and Latin-based words, we go beyond step 17.

2.4   Case study

Assessment data were from a pupil seven years of age, who was significantly behind in reading. The student was only just beginning to receive special assistance with reading at the school – see Table 2.4.

Lower case letter names and sounds – score was 21/26 letter names and 19/26 letter-sounds. Sounds not known were *y, v, u, l, h, w,* and *q*. The pupil confused some letter-sounds, e.g., the sound of *y* as /weh/ instead of /y/ and *h* as /ch/ instead of /h/. Recommended action – use alpha pictures to help with tricky letter-sounds – see Figure 2.2. Keep practising all 26 letter-sounds until perfect and fast.

Phonemic awareness – score was 19 out of 42. The benchmark score for this age level would be 36/42 correct. Possible action – activities such as finding pictures on the alphabet chart (see Figure 3.3 in Chapter 3), such as "Point to the pictures that end with /g/" (e.g., *dog* and *frog*). Use games like "I Spy something that starts with the sound …." Practise blending, e.g., "What word is /f-a-n/?" Practise segmenting, e.g., "What are the three sounds in /rug/?"

Alien Words Test (non-words) – score was 0/50. The benchmark for this age would be 30 non-words correct out of 50. Recommended action – start with simple phonics patterns (see Figure 3.3 in Chapter 3), practise reading and spelling consonant-vowel-consonant (CVC) words on the alphabet chart sidebar, e.g., *ant* and *mop*. Once the student can fluently identify the 26 letter-sounds, then practise reading and spelling Set 1 high frequency words (see Figure 3.15 in Chapter 3).

Burt Word Reading Test – the score on this normed test was one word correct. This was below the six-year-old level.

Graded passage – oral reading of a story – the student read 6 words out of 26. Words correctly read were *a, cat, to, the, I*.

Teaching plan – Chapter 3 has a scope and sequence for teaching decoding skills (Table 3.1) and resources the teacher can use (e.g., Figure 3.3). For this student it is best to start with the Figure 3, Set 1 letter-sounds "satp." Show how to decode words with combinations of the "satp" letter-sounds, e.g., *at, sat, pat, sad,* and *mad.* When these four letter-sounds in Set 1 are secure, i.e., when the student can read and spell words with "satp," move to the next set of four letter-sounds, and so on.

When identification of the 26 letter-sounds is perfect, introduce List 1 high frequency words. Keep practising. Make imaginary sentences out of the List 1 words, e.g., *dad got in the back.*

Follow a step-by-step teaching approach with the Scope and Sequence chart in Figure 2.1, starting with the 26 letter-sounds, then consonant digraphs, r- and l-affected vowels, split digraphs, chameleon letters c, g, y, and one- and two-sound vowel digraphs. This will take the student through to about an 8-year-level of reading skill.

If possible, introduce decodable books to reinforce and practise the rules. Most publishers, e.g., *Sunshine Phonics Decodables series* and *Little Learners Love Literacy,* follow the scope and sequence that you are teaching.

Imagine you are teaching this student, step by step, practising until perfect. Then one day the student's astonished parents announce to you that their child, who had eschewed reading for so long, is now reading! It can be done.

Table 2.4 Case Study Results for Checks of Letter Names, Letter Sounds, Phonemic Awareness, Alien Words Test, Burt Word Reading Test, and Graded Passage.

Assessment		*Comments*
Letter names	Uppercase – 22/26	Upper names unknown – J, U, V, Y
	Lowercase – 21/26	Lower names unknown – y, v, u, g, q
Letter–sounds	Uppercase – 20/26	Upper sounds unknown – L, H, W, Q
	Lowercase – 18/26	(kyeh), V, Y
		Lower sounds unknown – y (weh), v, i, u, h (ch), i, w, q (kyeh)
Phonemic awareness	Segmentation – 6/7	Subtest scores indicated ability to blend
	Blending – 7/7	and segment sounds which is a positive
	Initial Deletion – 3/7	predictor for reading but the student had
	Final Deletion – 3/7	difficulty with advanced tests of deletion
	Initial substitution – 0/7	and substitution
	Final Substitution – 0/7	
	Raw score – 19/42	
Alien words test	Raw score – 0/50	Unable to read simple non-words such as *buf* and *dit*
Burt word reading test	Raw score – 2	Expected raw score for this age level = 33
	Reading age – below 6 years	Words known – to, up
		Unknown words on first two lines of Burt test were – is, for, big, he, at, one, my, sun
Graded passage – simple story about a cat	Raw score – 6 words out of 26	Story was at a 6-year level. Correct words read aloud were *a, cat, to, the, I.* Decoding errors included *my/me, house/ here, she/said.*

Figure 2.2 Alpha Pictures

2.5   Conclusion

Assessment data can be very helpful to the teacher. They can give insights into current reading levels and possible areas for further teaching. These data help the teacher to design effective teaching.

Be sure to remember that assessment is not about evaluation; it is not about judging if they are skilled or unskilled at decoding. The assessments are to help the teacher understand where the student is coming from.

In every classroom, the teacher is teaching, but are students learning? Learning to decode well is about production. The student may be sitting up in class and receiving instruction, but is that translating into production? Assessment is to find out. Students may say they can decode words and may think they have the relevant skills, but only a careful assessment will tell whether they are on the right track.

3   Teaching decoding

3.1   Introduction

Decoding skill is the ability to read words accurately and fluently using grapheme-phoneme correspondences. It enables the reader to convert written text into its spoken form. It is a foundation skill because once children can decode the text they can then use their language comprehension knowledge to understand the ideas in the text. Decoding skill is the foundation of reading. It is a catalyst to enable children to read well.

This chapter will cover the following topics:

- A scope and sequence of decoding skills for the early years
- Teaching phonemic awareness skills
- A step by step approach to teaching decoding skills
- Should we teach high frequency words? Yes but not by rote memory

3.2   A scope and sequence of decoding skills for the early years

It is important to set goals for teaching decoding skills but what should we expect children to achieve at ages 5–8? The decoding skills continuum in Figure 3.1 gives

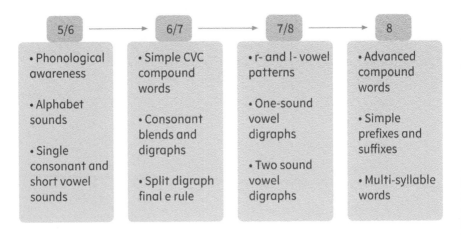

Figure 3.1 A Decoding Continuum for ages 5–8

DOI: 10.4324/9781003130758-4

some suggested achievement expectations at each age level. There is no reason why the teacher cannot go beyond these expectations in any one school year, depending on the class. These are minimum expectations. If children have not achieved these minimum goals at each age level, then the teacher must begin to ask questions – why is this? Why is the programme not working for all of them?

The scope and sequence in Table 3.1 is a conservative series of steps to follow. The NSW Department of Education (NSW Centre for Effective Reading, n.d.) has a similar scope and sequence, as does *Letters and Sounds* (Department for Education and Skills, 2007) used in the UK. We have tried to keep the scope and sequence achievable and not too technical – see also the 17 steps of the "decoding snake" in Chapter 2, Figure 2.1.

Table 3.1 Scope and Sequence – Decoding Skills, Ages 5–8.

Age 5–6	Age 6–7	Age 7–8	Age 8
Knows all 26 letter-sounds, e.g., *s-a-t-p* ... Knows how to read VC and CVC words, e.g., *at, in, up, sat, tap, fox* Knows all consonant clusters, e.g., *pram, milk*	Knows the main consonant digraphs, e.g., *chick, ship, thick, song, when* Knows the split digraph (final e) rule, e.g., *cake, kite* Knows the doubling rule for short vowel sounds, e.g., hoping-*hopping*	Knows the main r- and l-controlled vowel sounds, e.g., *ar, or, ur, er, ir, al* Knows the one-sound vowel digraphs, e.g., *ee, ai, oa* Knows the two-sound vowel digraphs, e.g., *ea, ou, ow, oo,*	Knows alternate sounds of *c, g, y,* e.g., *circus, giant, jelly* Knows compound word patterns e.g., *cup/cake, rain/coat* Knows simple prefixes and suffixes, e.g., *reread, baker* Knows simple grammatical inflections -*s, -ed, -ing* Knows the six syllable rules, e.g., *closed, open*

3.3 Teaching phonemic awareness

It is difficult to learn letter-sounds if you do not know what a "sound" is. The teacher can teach children about sounds by showing how to make the sounds with their lips, tongue, and mouth – see Figure 3.2. First, draw a "fish" shape on the whiteboard. To make the /p/ sound, the teacher draws the fish lips together and explains that the air "pops" out as a /p/. Phonemes like this are "popping" sounds /p b k d g t/. To make the /sh/ sound, the fish puts its tongue towards the front of the mouth and releases air slowly like the air in a tyre. These are "shooshy" sounds /sh s h f j z th v/. To make the /w/ sound, the fish keeps its mouth open. These are "wowey" sounds /y w r l/. To make the /n/ sound, the fish makes air go through its nose. These are "nosey" sounds /m n ng/. In Figure 3.2, the chart has drawings of different "fish" making the phoneme sound for each alphabet letter.

Lack of phonemic awareness, for many children, is maybe one of the biggest stumbling blocks in learning to read. This is because when you read words, you have to map the letters in each word to their sounds, but if you cannot do this, if

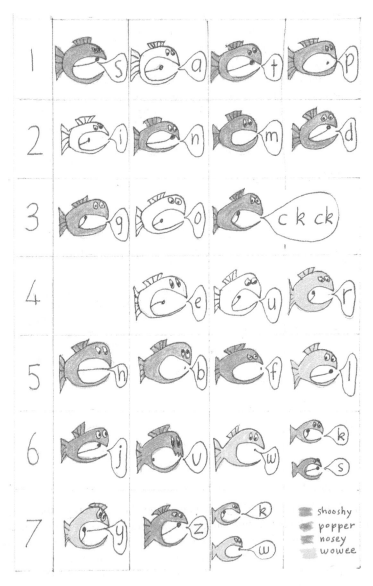

Figure 3.2 How to Make the Phoneme Sounds

you do not know what the teacher means by "sound," then you are blocked. Some children have this skill when they start school, but many do not. If you ask them to tell you the sounds in /cat/, they are likely to say /meow/.

If children have phonemic awareness, their answers are totally different. They can blend phonemes to make words, e.g., they know that /c-a-t/ says /cat/. They can segment the three sounds in /cat/ and say them /k-a-t/. They can delete the /k/ in /cat/ and say what is left /at/, and they can delete the last sound in /cat/ and say what is left /ca/. They can substitute phonemes; they can replace /k/ with /s/ to make /sat/ and replace /t/ with /p/ to make /cap/.

Some say that simply the process of teaching the letter-sounds of the alphabet (the ABCs) also teaches phonemic awareness because children learn that each letter has a sound (phoneme). Others argue that is like an insurance policy to teach awareness first. Whatever approach we take, whether teaching the letter-sounds first or phonemic awareness first, the main thing is to check that the phoneme thing is happening. If children are confused, then best to teach phonemic awareness. It is easy to teach this. Using the chart in Figure 3.3, the teacher can ask students to find drawings on the chart that end with the same sound, e.g., *dog, log, jug* all end with /g/. The teacher can ask students to find drawings on the chart that start with the same sound, e.g., *keg, cat, queen* all start with /k/.

The teacher can point to certain drawings on the chart and ask children to segment the sounds, e.g., rug (3), up (2), frog (4), and box (4). The teacher can choose a drawing on the chart without saying what it is, e.g., the drawing of the duck, and then slowly blend the phonemes, e.g., /d-u-ck/. Children have to say what word it is, in this case, /duck/. To teach the spelling process, the teacher points to three drawings on the chart, e.g., *rug, ant*, and *tin* and encourages children to think of what word the initial phonemes spell, /rat/. The pictures *pot, egg*, and *gun* – their initial phonemes spell /peg/.

Phonemic awareness is not enough on its own to work out the letter-sound rules of English writing but it is a necessary part of the puzzle – it is a prerequisite. Necessary but not sufficient. There is much variance in student phonemic awareness at school entry, and teaching can improve these skills. If teaching time is short, a suggestion to the teacher of beginner readers is to focus on just two phonemic awareness skills – blending and segmenting.

3.4 Teaching decoding skills

The 26 letter-sounds – and consonant clusters

Figure 3.3 is a chart of the 26 letter-sounds. In the chart, on the first line, are four letter-sounds s-a-t-p. When they know these four letter-sounds, s-a-t-p, children can start to read and spell words like *at, sat, pat, tap, sap*. They are learning the alphabetic principle, they are learning to decode words.

Be sure to teach the 26 letter-sounds so there is minimal distortion. For example, for *s-a-t-p* in Set 1 of the chart in Figure 3.3, try to say letter-sound /s/ as a continuous sound /s/, not as /seh/. In the case of the letter-sound *a*, the phoneme is /a/ as in *at*. For the letter sound *t*, it is hard to say its sound without distortion but try to say /t/ not /teh/. For the letter-sound *p*, try to say /p/ not /peh/. Some children add /eh/ to the letter-sounds when they go through the alphabet, but they need to blend the letter-sounds as one continuous sound when they decode words, e.g., /s-a-t/ not /seh-uh-teh/.

A feature of the Set 1 letters *s a t p* is that it is possible to create five to six words from just those four letters *at, sat, pat, tap, taps, sap*. This helps students get off to a very quick start in reading words.

The chart in Figure 3.3 has regular three-letter words on the sidebar made from the 26 letter-sounds for them to practise their word reading. Children need to practise the letter-sounds and the sidebar words on the chart until they are automatic, i.e., they can read the sidebar words on the chart fluently and quickly and spell them quickly and accurately.

The teacher can help children to go beyond three-letter words as well, to read words with clusters like *st*, *bl*, and *tw*. Students can practise words like *clock*, *plug*, *twins*, and *steps*.

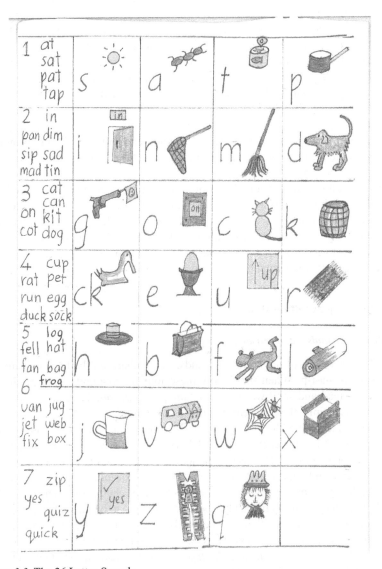

Figure 3.3 The 26 Letter-Sounds

Consonant digraphs

The chart in Figure 3.4 has the main consonant digraphs for beginners, *ch sh th ng*. Each digraph has two letters that usually make **one** sound. The digraphs *wh* and *ph* can come later in the programme. The Anglo-Saxon scribes created consonant digraphs because there were sounds in Anglo-Saxon not represented by letters in the Roman alphabet. They added *h* to some letters to form the new sounds. These digraphs (except -ng) can be at the beginning or end of a word. The digraph *th* has a voiced (e.g., *the*) and unvoiced sound (e.g., *thin*).

Figure 3.4 is a teaching chart to practise decoding words with these consonant digraphs, e.g., *chick, ship, the/thin, song*. Keep practising until fluent.

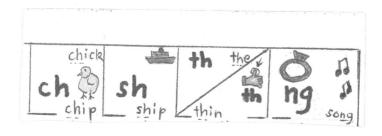

I sang a song in the chip shop.
The moth is on the cloth.
The ant is in the shed.
The brick is thick.
The dog had chops and the cat
had chicken.
The fish shop had hot chips.
I am going on the bus.
The big ship is at the dock.

Figure 3.4 Consonant Digraphs

Split digraph (final e rule)

A *vowel digraph* is two vowel letters making one sound. A *split digraph* (or final e rule) is a conditional spelling rule where the final e has no sound of its own but signals that the preceding vowel has its long sound, as in words like *lake*, *bike*, *hope*, *cube*, and *Pete*.

One way to illustrate the split digraph rule is to use a same-different lesson design, showing how the vowel sound changes from short to long using the final e as a marker, e.g., *at-ate, kit-kite, cut-cute, hop-hope,* and *pet-Pete.*

In the past, teachers have made up many names for this marking rule such as *silent e* and *magic e*. The term split digraph, or final e rule, is more descriptive of how the rule works, but children may like other ways to describe the split digraph, such as "silent e" or "magic e."

It is a useful rule so it is worth spending time on it. Figure 3.5 is a teaching chart with examples of the split digraph rule.

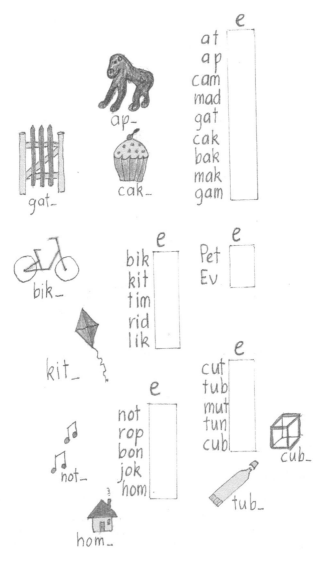

Figure 3.5 Split Digraph (Final e) Rule

r- and l-controlled vowel sounds

Figures 3.6–3.8 give examples of this pattern. The five short vowel sounds change their sounds if followed by /r/. The effects are a normal part of speech, of articulation. In teaching the r-affected vowel sounds, a suggestion is to start with *ar, or, ur*. Later, do *ir, er*. Finally, do *air, ear, ure*. Note there are three different spellings of the /er/ sound *ur, ir,* and *er*. The most important I-affected

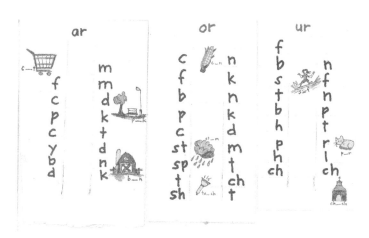

Figure 3.6 The R-affected Vowel Sounds AR-OR-UR

Figure 3.7 The R-affected vowel sounds IR-ER-AIR-EAR-URE

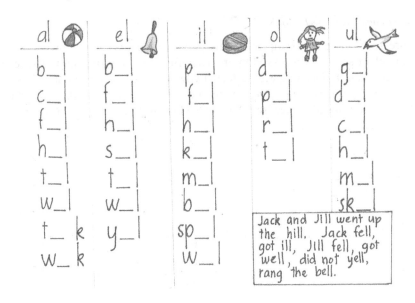

Figure 3.8 The L-affected Vowel Sounds AL-IL-EL-OL-UL

vowel sound to teach is the *–al* pattern. It changes the vowel sound to /or/, as in *tall* and *talk*.

One-sound vowel digraphs

Figures 3.9 and 3.10 give examples of this rule. A one-sound vowel digraph is two vowels together making one vowel sound, e.g., *ai* represents the long /a/

Figure 3.9 One-sound Vowel Digraphs AI-EE-OA

sound, as in *sail*. Teaching – There are some points that are useful to know, e.g., that we usually spell the /ay/ sound as *ai* in the middle of the word and *ay* at the end.

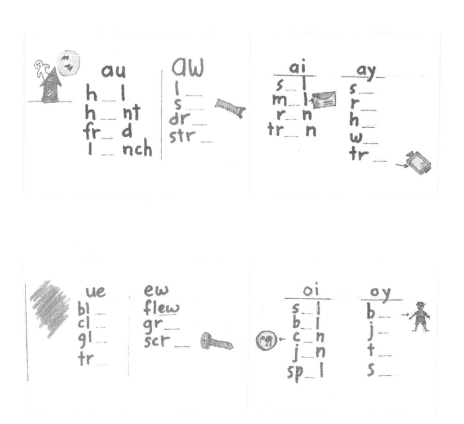

Figure 3.10 One-sound Vowel Digraphs AU-AW-UE-EW

Two-sound vowel digraphs

Figures 3.11 and 3.12 illustrate this rule. A two-sound vowel digraph is two vowels together that represent two different vowel sounds, e.g., *ea* in *leaf* and *bread*, *oo* in moon and *book*. Two-sound digraphs occur in 15% of words (Stanback, 1992).

Figure 3.11 Two-sound Vowel Digraphs EA-IE-OU

oo

t ___
b ___
z ___
r ___ m
r ___ m
m ___ n
f ___ n
f ___ d
t ___ th

OO

c ___ k
b ___ k
f ___ t
s ___ t
w ___ d
g ___ d
cr ___ k

ow

c ___
h ___
n ___
d ___ n
cl ___ n
br ___ l
gr ___

OW

t ___
m ___
l ___
bl ___
cr ___
gl ___
thr ___

ei

eight
weigh
sleigh
vein
freight
neighbour
reindeer

ei

seize
receive
protein
either
caffeine

Figure 3.12 Two-sound Vowel Digraphs OO-OW-EI

Chameleon letters – c, g, y

Figure 3.13 illustrates this rule. The consonants *c, g,* and *y* can each have two sounds depending on what letters come after them. The rule is

1. c sounds like /s/ when it comes in front of *e, i,* and *y* and sounds like /k/ elsewhere
2. g sounds like /j/ when it comes in front of *e, i,* and *y* and sounds like /g/ elsewhere
3. y at the end of a word is a vowel sound – it has two sounds as in *my, baby*

Teaching – explain that for letters c and g the sound depends on what comes after it. If it is *e, i,* or *y,* the c and g change sound. For y, explain it has a consonant sound at the start of the word but a vowel sound at the end of the word.

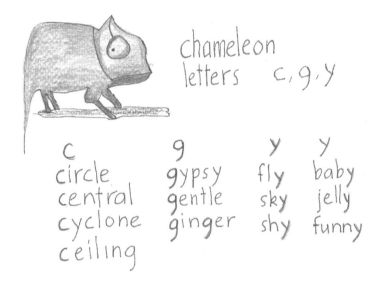

Figure 3.13 Chameleon Letter-Sounds C, G, Y

Simple compound words

A compound word is two real words joined together. Sometimes a compound word means what it says, e.g., *footstep*, but sometimes it only partly means what it says, e.g., *strawberry*. A simple CVC compound word is *laptop*, but a more complex spelling might be *raincoat, snowman*. The teacher might demonstrate to the class how the compound word is two real words and draw a line in the middle, e.g., *lap/top, rain/coat*.

Simple prefixes and suffixes – grammatical inflections and morphemes

Morphemes are the smallest units of meaning in a word, and prefixes are small units of meaning at the start of the word, e.g., *pre-* means before, *ex-* means out, *a-* indicates direction as in *away*.

Suffixes come at the end of a word and can have meaning, e.g., the *-er* means "someone who does something" as in *climb-er*. Suffixes also can change the part of speech, e.g., to an adverb as in *sadly*, to past tense, as in *jumped*, to the plural form, as in *dogs*.

Compound words and multi-syllable words

Compound words were very common in Anglo-Saxon spelling, where two existing words combine to create a new word, e.g., *foot-path* and *king-fish*.

Multi-syllable words are words with two or more syllables. To decode a multi-syllable word, the steps are as follows:

1. Check off the vowel sounds. Every syllable has one vowel sound, e.g., for *magnetic*, we check off three vowel sounds.
2. Put a line between each syllable. Where you put the line depends on the type of syllable. If there are two consonants dividing the two syllables, we split between them, e.g., *mag/net* and *cot/ton*.
3. Blend the syllables together to pronounce the word.

The chart in Figure 3.14 has examples of the six syllable rules that operate in multi-syllable words. Teach children the different patterns and how to break them into syllables. Practise the chart until fluent. There are six different syllable types:

- A closed syllable (short vowel sound), divide between the two consonants, e.g., *ra<u>b</u>-<u>b</u>it*
- An open syllable (long vowel sound), divide after the first vowel, e.g., *r<u>o</u>/bot*
- An r-affected vowel syllable, divide after the *r*, e.g., *j<u>er</u>/kin*
- A vowel digraph syllable, keep the two vowels together, *e.g., f<u>oo</u>/lish*
- A split digraph syllable, remember the final e is not a separate sound, e.g., *trom/b<u>o</u>n<u>e</u>*
- A consonant + -le syllable, keep the consonant + -le together, e.g., *nee/<u>dle</u>, jug/<u>gle</u>*

Figure 3.14 Multi-syllable Words

3.5   High frequency words ("sight words")

Teaching high frequency words (or sight words) is a daily routine for many teachers like having a cup of tea or coffee at morning break. It is a regular part of the daily routine. The teacher puts up a chart of sight words and children chant out the names of the words in unison. But is this the right way to learn for them to learn high frequency words?

Learning words this way may unwittingly focus too much on learning to remember words visually. In one classroom we observed, the beginner readers would read out loud each day 10–12 high frequency words on a chart. Each chart was named after an animal. The tiger words chart included *good, little*, and *bread*. The frog words chart included *looking, children, girls, naughty*. The monkey words chart included *birthday, liked, for, lunch*. It was rote learning. In terms of decoding patterns, it was a jumble. Many of the words on the charts were not high frequency words but were interest words. The lessons were well intentioned but were they sending the message that the only way to learn to read words is to memorise them? It is not necessary to do this. When we look carefully at high frequency words, it is clear that most of them can be decoded. Even words with tricky spellings can be sounded out to some extent. The 100 most frequent words in English account for 50% of the words children read (and write). Most of the words have regular spellings – about 60%, and the other 40% are partly irregular and called "tricky" words. There is a better way to teach such words, as in the UK's *Letters and Sounds* (Department for Education and Skills, 2007). What they did was split the 100 words into four sets, starting with the easiest to spell and read, words that beginners could easily sound out using their decoding skills.

The four sets of words are in Figure 3.15. A suggestion is to start with the Set 1 words. Teach Sets 2–4 later, when children have more advanced decoding skills and know how to read words with consonant digraphs, vowel digraphs, and the past tense ending, -ed. Teach the tricky words separately from the regularly spelled words.

The Set 1 words in Figure 3.15 are mostly two- and three-letter words. There are 25 regularly spelled words and 6 tricky words. The regular words include *a, as, if, is, off, on, an, dad, mum, but*, and *get*. The tricky spellings include *I, no, go, to, the*, and *into*. The tricky words on the chart have a red border. The regular words have a blue border. Children should practise these until fluent.

The Set 2 words in Figure 3.15 are mostly four-letter words. There are 15 regularly spelled words and 9 tricky words. The regular words are *will, that, this, then, them, with, see, for, now, down, look, too, her, you*, and *all*. The regular spellings include the consonant digraph *th*, vowel digraphs *ee, oo, ow, ou*, the r-controlled vowels *or, er*, and l-controlled vowel sound *-al*. The tricky words are *he, she, we, me, be, was, they, are, my*.

The Set 3 words in Figure 3.16 are mostly four-letter words. There are nine regularly spelled words and 11 tricky words. The regular words are *went, it's, from, children, just, help, when, out*, and *like*. The regular spellings include consonant clusters *went* and *just*, consonant digraphs *ch* and *wh*, a contraction, *it's*, and the split digraph *like*. The tricky words are *so, do, said, have, some, come, were, there, little, one*, and *what*.

The Set 4 words in Figure 3.16 are mostly four-letter words, but some have five and six letters. There are 12 regularly spelled words and 13 tricky words. The regular words are *don't, old, I'm, by, time, house, saw, about, day, made, came, make*. The tricky words are *put, oh, their, people, here, very, Mr, Mrs, your, could, looked, called, asked*. The regular spellings in the list include vowel digraphs *ou, aw, ay*, split digraphs *i-e* and *a-e*, contractions *I'm* and *don't*. Tricky words include *their, here, people, could, Mr, Mrs, your, very, oh, put*. Three words in the tricky list have the *-ed* past tense inflection, *looked, called, asked*. Although these three words have regular spellings, children may not yet have studied morpheme endings and so at this early stage they are regarded as "tricky."

a	as	if	is	off
on	an	at	in	it
up	dad	had	and	big
his	got	mum	can	get
not	him	but	back	of

1

I	no	go
to	the	into

2

will	that	this	then
them	with	see	for
now	down	look	too
her	you	all	

2

he	she	we	me
be	was	they	are
my			

Figure 3.15 High Frequency Words – Sets 1 and 2

3			
went	it's	from	children
just	help	when	out
like			

3			
so	do	said	have
some	come	were	there
little	one	what	

4			
don't	old	I'm	by
time	house	saw	about
day	made	came	make

4			
put	oh	their	people
here	very	Mr	Mrs
your	could		
looked	called	asked	

Figure 3.16 High Frequency Words – Sets 3 and 4

3.6   Conclusion

It is important for the teacher to follow a structured scope and sequence to teach decoding skills explicitly on a regular basis. Some children when they start school are linguistically ready to learn the letter-sound rules of English writing, that is, they have phonemic awareness but many children may not have this preparation so it is worth giving some phonemic awareness instruction to the class either before or while teaching the 26 letter-sounds. This will set up the whole class for further learning. It will lay the foundation to learn the other decoding rules.

The 100 high frequency words do have some parts that require the child to memorise them as "exceptions" to the rule. It is important to teach the 100 words in four separate sets, one set at a time. Only go to the next set if children are fluent in the words for that set. Most of the 100 words are regular in spelling with just one part of the word that is an exception to the rule. The message to the class is that their decoding skills will help them with these words; they should not rely on memory for the visual look of the words.

Learning the letter-sound rules does not happen overnight; there will be speed bumps along the way. The scope and sequence chart is the key to step by step effective teaching. Sometimes depending on the class, the pace has to slow down, and there has to be more practice so as to build confidence, and then to move on. The teacher needs to be flexible so that no children are left by the wayside.

Part II

Reading Comprehension

4 Reading comprehension

What is it?

4.1 Introduction

To comprehend well, the reader needs multi-component skills. They need to de-code well, and they need a depth of vocabulary, grammar, and background knowl-edge. This is no easy task, and it shows up in national assessment results.

The most recent NAPLAN results (Australian Curriculum, Assessment and Reporting Authority, n.d.) for Year 3 children (8.5 years old) showed much vari-ance in reading comprehension across sub-groups. Of concern were the results for Indigenous children and for children whose parents did not complete senior sec-ondary education, only 35% of these students met or exceeded expectations. For Indigenous children in very remote locations, only 8% met or exceeded expecta-tions. In contrast, for children whose parents had university degrees, 81% met or exceeded expectations.

How do we close this gap? It is hard for teachers to move the needle on compre-hension (Willingham, 2023–2024), but we think that children, with help from their teachers, can drive their own comprehension progress. In this chapter, we explain how and why.

This chapter covers the following topics:

- Defining reading comprehension
- The need for background knowledge
- The need to ask questions
- The need to engage the reader
- Research on teaching comprehension
- Narrative text
- Expository text
- The CORE model

4.2 Definition

A simple definition of reading comprehension is the process of understanding any communication that is in writing, whether it be books, letters, Twitter/Facebook/Instagram, billboards, road signs, package labels, and so on. A more in-depth

DOI: 10.4324/9781003130758-6

definition of reading comprehension is that it is the process of extracting information from text and constructing meaning from it. This process involves both the literal information in the text (the lines) and the unstated but implied meaning (between the lines) and meaning that the reader must access from their prior knowledge (beyond the lines).

4.3   The need for background knowledge

Although many children have a base of language skills on starting school, they will need more. Much of what they will read requires a depth of background knowledge. There is no question that having relevant background knowledge about the subject increases comprehension (Shanahan, n.d.; Willingham, 2006-2007).

Background knowledge is schema knowledge, or knowledge of the world. Catts (2021-22, p. 28) wrote, "A schema is an organized unit of knowledge that forms the foundation for many activities involving human thought." Schema theory describes the kind of background knowledge that students need to bring to the text to understand it (McVee et al., 2005).

The thing about mental schema in long-term memory is that it is organised knowledge, not a jumble of random facts. Teachers can help students to develop more and more elaborate schema, or world knowledge. Research on schema theory in the 1970s (e.g., Anderson, 1978; Pearson & Johnson, 1978) enabled researchers to discover what is obvious now, the huge importance of background knowledge in comprehension.

Skilled readers bring more background (i.e., prior) knowledge to the text than do unskilled readers. Background knowledge is mostly content knowledge about all sorts of things, e.g., spiders, camping, kangaroos, bedtime, and zoos.

If the reader is reading about the monarch butterfly and they have a lot of background knowledge about this insect, it is much more likely the reader will comprehend in detail what they read. In contrast, if the reader is reading about snow sledding yet has never experienced snow (or sledding) then they are less likely to understand the text.

Why do students often lack relevant background knowledge? Some students may not have experienced the beach, mountain, snow, or lakes. Some students may not have eaten popcorn or pineapple or gone camping. For young readers teachers will need to build background knowledge about any unfamiliar content prior to reading.

At a school that one of the authors visited, the seven-year-old students would visit the library to build background knowledge prior to learning a new topic. For example, for a new topic the teacher wanted to cover on *insects*, when they visited the library, the librarian would focus on insects. Alternatively, if students were going to be learning about the Australian gold rushes, the librarian or teacher would begin to build background knowledge two weeks prior to the unit commencing. It takes time to build necessary prior knowledge, and teachers play an important role in doing so. Reading multiple texts on the same topic is a way of building background knowledge.

Experiences are a practical way to build background knowledge. We can read about lakes, rivers, and the sea, but watching relevant television documentaries, videos, and programmes on the internet or visiting these places in person are powerful ways to enhance background knowledge. We can read about making popcorn, but watching someone making it on YouTube or having children make popcorn themselves is a powerful way to gain a depth of background knowledge.

Students need background knowledge for comprehension. Imagine reading an article about cricket if you were unfamiliar with terms such as wicket, stumps, bails, maiden over, batting collapse, or dead ball. Comprehension would be difficult if these terms (and others unknown to the reader) were in the text. Imagine if the class have never experienced a sheep farm or sheep but have to read an article about shearing of sheep. It could be very confusing especially if it went into any detail about farms and sheep. Teachers can anticipate these issues and build background knowledge prior to reading.

These teaching activities to build background will certainly help with specific texts but for most students to build a width and depth of background knowledge, it will take years of schooling, extensive reading, outside experiences, watching educational programmes, etc. For this reason, encouraging students to do extensive reading of books and other media should be a major focus of reading comprehension instruction in that it will help to build general knowledge (Carver, 1987). For children who do not have fluent decoding skills, they can still "read" extensively if they read along and listen to audio text. They should not be left out of the opportunity for extensive reading. They also need background knowledge.

4.4   Self-questioning

Questioning involves the reader actively asking and answering questions as they read. It is not the teacher asking the students questions, rather the students actively asking and answering their own questions as they read. We can do more to encourage children to ask questions about the content/subject matter and ask questions about the text structure. Joseph et al. (2016) reviewed 48 studies on self-questioning with children aged 8–9 years and found that

- Teachers can demonstrate how to ask questions, provide guided practice, and give feedback
- Asking questions to yourself while reading has a positive effect on comprehension
- Self-questioning enhances performance on comprehension tests

4.5   Engagement

In theory, a well-written text should be engaging, inspiring, and entertaining – but to engage students the text has to mean something to them and link with their prior knowledge. Teachers play an important role in engaging students. A story that features feta cheese sandwiches may not mean a lot to a young student who has not experienced feta cheese. This student may immediately tune out when the teacher starts discussing a story about the boy who took feta cheese sandwiches to school. No background knowledge can result in no engagement. What can teachers do? Prior to reading the story, the teacher could share some feta cheese with the children. This will help to engage all students – whether they are familiar with feta cheese or not. Imagine a reading lesson beginning with feeling, smelling, and/or tasting feta cheese.

Teachers cannot provide experiences for every topic that students read about, but there are many opportunities to engage students so as to get them excited about books. If every lesson began with an exciting hook to reel in the class straight away and have them itching to read the book with the teacher, if we engaged them, grabbed their attention, and had them all looking at the teacher, on tenterhooks, would we have a generation of readers, passionate about books? Absolutely. Engagement also links to background knowledge. If we are interested in a topic, we will store in memory as much detail as we can about it.

Of course, the mind can only process so much. Many texts that children read are full of information that will be lost unless the mind does something to structure it. Children can only hold in memory a limited amount of information at any one time, but if they can engage with the text and bring background knowledge to the text, it will reduce the cognitive load and lead to more effective learning.

4.6   Research on teaching comprehension

Although there is much current emphasis on reading comprehension, teachers did not always teach it. Durkin's (1978-1979) classic study involved visiting many classrooms. She found that teachers devoted very little time in direct, explicit instruction to enhance reading comprehension. To Durkin, teaching comprehension was saying something to help children understand or work out the meaning of more than a single, isolated word. What she found after observing 30 classes in 14 schools for 193 hours was that only a total of 45 minutes was spent teaching reading comprehension. The 45 minutes occurred over 12 separate episodes with the average length of each episode being 3.7 minutes. You are probably wondering what the teachers were doing during instructional reading time. Durkin's analysis of their teaching was that teachers were busy but not directly teaching. She categorised them as follows:

- Mentioners, i.e., saying just enough so students could get on with the task
- Assignment checkers, i.e., making sure students had completed the set task
- Assignment givers, i.e., giving students worksheets or assignments to complete
- Interrogators, i.e., asking questions and drilling down to check comprehension

This tendency for teachers to give little time to actual comprehension instruction may still be the case. Some 20 years after Durkin's findings, the RAND report (Snow, 2002) found that "studies of classroom practice are unanimous in noting the scarcity of time devoted to comprehension instruction" (p. 44). They found that teaching of reading comprehension was "often minimal," and if reading comprehension was taught, the report found it was "ineffective" (p. 5).

Durkin's research did, however, have a positive influence in that it has led to many more research articles and books on teaching reading comprehension (e.g., Block & Parris, 2008; Block & Pressley, 2002, 2003; Duke et al., 2021; Dymock, 2005, 2007, 2017; Dymock & Nicholson, 2012; Pressley, 2008; Pressley et al., 2023).

Even when teachers do allocate significant time to teaching comprehension, it is a major challenge for the teacher to teach it effectively. Summarising and creating graphic organisers helps students to gain a better understanding of specific texts but may not help children to make gains on standardised tests (Filderman et al., 2022; Hwang et al., 2023; Okkinga et al., 2018). There is some transfer but not very much. Why is that? The problem is that to do well on a standardised test the student needs a huge and extensive amount of general knowledge. The only way students can gain the knowledge base necessary to succeed in standardised tests is through extensive reading and classroom instruction. Comprehension lessons help a little but not enough.

The teacher can teach the class to find the main points in a text, to locate background knowledge relevant to the text, but this is only going to help students understand one text. It will not transfer to the next text they read which may be on a totally different topic. It is up to the student to do the extensive reading needed to build sufficient knowledge of the world to do well on general tests of knowledge like NAPLAN. This takes time.

4.7   Teaching text structure, how it fits the mind of the reader

Text structure is a key to reading comprehension success but even many skilled readers do not know much about text structure. Does this matter? It does in the sense that students can read without fully understanding what is happening. Reading comprehension is not the same as riding a bike; in riding a bike you do not need to know how it was built. With reading comprehension, though, it does help to know how texts are built.

It means understanding a story not just as a story but to see it in the same way as an architect, as a construction, and as a design. To see the structure of the text is to see the writer in action and to see the tools they use to construct text. It is seeing the bigger picture, and this is helpful when thinking about text and writing text.

To the adult, this may seem obvious, but often it is not obvious to the student. They can enjoy a story but lack the academic language to talk about its parts, to be able to talk about what made it an enjoyable story. Many children do not know the technical elements of a story, that it has character/s, plot, and setting.

It is the same with expository text. Imagine if you read an expository text but all you saw was a list of facts with no apparent connection (e.g., elephants are large, Antarctica is cold, Australia is large, Darwin is warm, Bali is a holiday destination, puppies like to chew, and oranges are citrus). You are seeing one side of the text but not how it was made, not how it was made interesting.

A big advantage to learning about text structure is that it helps the mind to organise and store knowledge. There are so many details in a text, it is impossible to remember all of them. What we have to do is sort through the details and organise them, and this helps to remember the main elements. This is what text structure work does.

We cannot remember every detail. Short-term memory has a limited storage capacity in terms of amount of information, perhaps four to five chunks (Calfee, 1984; Miller, 1956). For this reason, it is important to focus on key points when reading. By looking at the text's structure, we can organise the details into a small number of chunks, and it will then be easier to remember and recall the meaning of the text.

4.8   Narrative text structure

Authors typically write narratives to entertain the reader. Most children enjoy listening to or reading a story. Stories in general are easier to understand than nonfiction text as they often reflect our everyday lives and experiences (e.g., going shopping, deciding on a family pet, bike riding, and baking a cake). Stories adhere to structure.

Research suggests that skilled readers, readers as young as six years old, have an understanding of the structure of stories and use this knowledge to comprehend. An example of this is a quote from Calfee (1991) of a six-year-old's take on story structure (p. 178):

> What you have to do with a story is you analyze it; you break it into parts. You figure out the characters, how they're the same and different. And the plot, how it begins with a problem and goes on until it is solved. Then you understand the story better, and you can even write your own.

Consider the knowledge this six-year-old student has gained about narratives. The student understands that stories have a structure, that stories have characters and a plot, and that this knowledge not only helps to comprehend stories, but it also helps to compose them.

Research in the 1970s found that stories/narratives had a common structure, a set of rules, called story grammar (Mandler & Johnson, 1977; Rumelhart, 1980). Story grammar is literally a set of rules, like the set of rules writers follow when constructing a sentence, for composing narratives. The rules are that stories must include a setting, characters, plot, and theme (Thorndyke, 1977).

The terminology of story grammar is complex but the teacher can simplify it for young readers. A simple way to define "narrative" is to say that it is a story. Stories have a special structure:

- Stories have one or more **characters**, with either major roles or minor roles.
- Stories have a **setting**; they take place somewhere at a particular time.
- Stories have a **plot**, made up of one or more episodes, where characters face a challenge/problem, respond to the problem, do something about the problem, and there is an outcome.
- Stories have a **theme**, that is, a message intended for the reader, not always explicitly stated, that often requires the reader to "read between the lines."

Stories may have more than one theme/message. Stories may also have more than one episode. Each episode in the plot, however, has the same basic structure (problem, response, action, and outcome). One way for children to visualise the story structure is to draw up a "spider web" diagram that connects the four parts of a story: characters, setting, plot, and theme. This helps to "see" the building blocks of a story – as shown in Figure 4.1.

Story Web - Building Blocks of a Story

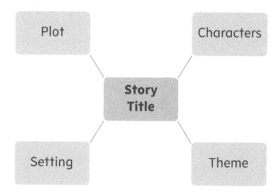

Figure 4.1 Story Web Structure

For younger children in the five to six age range, beginning to read, the best books to start with are contemporary decodable books (e.g., publishers like *Sunshine Phonics Decodables series* and *Little Learners Love Literacy*). For older children, reading picture books aloud will also work well, e.g., well-known picture books like *Edward the emu* (Knowles, 1988) and *John Brown, Rose and the midnight cat* (Wagner, 1977). The story lines in these books are easy to follow and excellent examples to use for showing structure.

Imagine the teacher has read to the class *Andrew and Sue make a kite* (Beattie, 2021). Here is the text of this decodable book (with permission, Wendy Pye Publishing Ltd)

"I would like to make a kite," said Andrew. Let's look at the computer and see how to do it," said Sue. They looked on the computer. "You read it" said Andrew "and tell me what to do." Sue said, "1. Cut out the kite 2: Cut out the tail 3: Get a tube of glue 4. Glue the kite on the wood 5: Put the tail on the kite 6: Glue on a string." Andrew said, "We could cut up the newspaper. Dad and Mum have finished it." Andrew drew the kite on the newspaper and did as Sue said. Then they looked at the kite Andrew had made. "Let me put blue on it," said Sue. "I'll put red on it," said Andrew. "Then we will have a blue and red newspaper kite." Sue put red and blue on the tail too. They had to wait while the kite dried. The children went to the park. Andrew threw the kite.

Up, up, up it went, into the blue sky. Andrew flew the kite. He had to run as it swooped up and down, up and down. "You have a go," Andrew said to Sue.

The kite swooped up and down, up and down. Sue had to run and run. It was a lot of fun. Then CRASH! The kite flew into a big tree. Oh dear! Oh dear. The kite was torn. "We will glue and fix it up," said Andrew, "and we will run with it again."

The teacher can show students how to diagram the story structure – see Figure 4.2. In terms of structure, the story had a **setting** – in the present day, at home, and at the local park. The **characters** were two young children, Andrew and Sue. The **theme** was that you can solve a problem if you work together as a team. The **plot** had two main episodes:

Episode 1

Problem – The children want to make a kite
Response – They face the challenge of how to make one
Action – They fly their kite
Outcome – Kite hits a large tree

Episode 2

Problem: The kite was torn.
Response: Sad
Action: They glue and fix up the kite
Outcome: They fly the kite

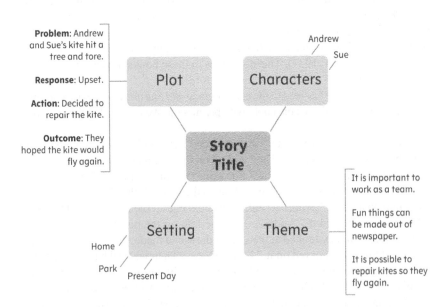

Figure 4.2 Story Web Structure for Andrew and Sue Make a Kite

4.9   Expository text structure

Expository text is more difficult than narrative for young readers to understand. This was the finding of Mar et al. (2021) who carried out a meta-analysis of 37 studies. This was a significant finding and has considerable implications for classroom teachers at all year levels.

Table 4.1 compares narrative and expository text in the school situation. It shows areas where expository text is more difficult for children. The main differences are as follows:

1. Expository text has many different structures.
2. There is a scarcity of expository text in junior classrooms.
3. Vocabulary is often technical, specialised.
4. Content is typically new.
5. Concepts can be abstract (e.g., electricity, water cycle, life cycle).

Table 4.1 Comparison of Narrative and Expository Text.

	Narrative	*Expository*
Structure	One main structure	Many different structures
Purpose	Tell a story	Explain content
Prevalence in school	Common	Uncommon
Vocabulary	Everyday	Technical
Content	Familiar	New
Comprehension	Easier	Harder

One reason why expository text is more difficult for students to comprehend is that schools often do not introduce it to them, not to any great extent, until the upper grades. Preschool children learn about narrative structure through storytelling from family members as well as from books read to them by their parents and at early childcare/kindergarten learning centres. They do not learn similar amounts about expository text. In short, the instructional material teachers teach to children in the early years is predominantly narrative (Duke, 2000). This explains why it is easier for children to make sense of. In contrast expository texts have very different structures. Expository (information) texts that young readers encounter at school are divided into two broad categories – texts that describe things (i.e., descriptive texts) and texts affected by time (i.e., sequential).

Descriptive texts

List

Some texts have a list structure; it is a list of the attributes of something, e.g., a list of objects, a list of jobs to do, a list of ingredients for a cake, a list of dreams that might come true – anything that can go on a list. It is rather like a shopping list. It does not matter what comes first in the list.

Web

Some texts have a web structure. They describe one topic or thing (e.g., butterflies, wombats, and Sydney). The web structure has several subtopics, e.g., for Sydney it might describe its history, population size, geographical location, main products, and tourist attractions.

Weave

Some texts have a weave structure that compares two or more things (e.g., butterflies and moths; kangaroos and wallabies; bees and wasps). The weave is an extension of the web structure. In a weave, instead of focusing on one animal, or one city, or one form of travel, the text compares and contrasts two or more. For example, the children's instructional reader, *Farms* (Iverson, 1995), for five to six year olds, compares and contrasts different kinds of farms, e.g., market garden, orchard, and wheat farm – see Figure 4.3.

Figure 4.3 Weave Structure for Different Kinds of Farms

Sequential texts

Linear string

Some texts follow a step-by-step sequence. This is the linear string pattern. It is probably the most frequently occurring structure that children read at ages 5–8 – see its generic structure in Figure 4.4.

The linear string structure has a set order. It matters what comes first. It is a first to last pattern. Examples of linear string would be activities such as making toast, brushing teeth, or milking a cow – see Figure 4.5 for the steps in milking a cow or getting dressed for school.

Cyclical

Some texts have a cyclical structure. It is circular such as showing the stages in the life cycle of a butterfly – see Figure 4.6. In this kind of text, the process keeps repeating itself. Other examples of a cyclical structure would be the water cycle, the seasons, the election cycle, and the poverty cycle.

Figure 4.4 Linear String Structure – Generic

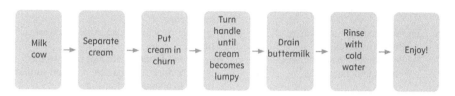

Figure 4.5 Linear string structure – Milking Cows

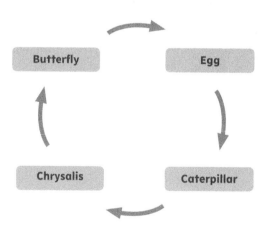

Figure 4.6 Cyclical Structure – Life Cycle of a Butterfly

4.10 The CORE model

The CORE model of instruction CORE (connect, organise, reflect, extend) was developed to assist teachers in lesson planning that is meaningful and engaging (Calfee & Patrick, 1995). Whether it is a short reading lesson or a unit of instruction in the content area (e.g., social studies, and science), lessons can follow the CORE model of instruction. The difference between the traditional classroom and the CORE classroom is that CORE focuses much more on explicit direct instruction – see Table 4.2.

Table 4.2 Comparing the Traditional Classroom with the CORE Approach.

	Traditional classroom	Modern classroom – CORE
1	Small group	Whole class
2	Ability groups	Mixed ability
3	Different book levels for each group	Whole class does same book – no different levels
4	Developing readers do low level tasks like worksheets whereas skilled readers do high level tasks	All readers do high level tasks – focus on comprehension
5	Before reading – predict, scan the text	**C**onnect – teacher links to background knowledge
6	During reading – students read silently or to teacher	**O**rganise – teacher creates visual diagrams of text
7	After reading – teacher checks general understanding	**R**eview and **E**xtend – teacher reviews the text structure, assigns new tasks on similar topics to encourage transfer

4.11   Conclusion

Comprehension requires the reader to decode the text, understand its individual word meanings, parse its sentences, create a mental discourse structure, and internalise it. Knowledge is an important factor in reading comprehension. Without relevant background knowledge, comprehension will be impaired. One key message is not to choose texts too difficult for children to read. It will only undermine their confidence. If it is too difficult, then read it aloud to them. The other key message is to teach text structure. It will help students to gain a better understanding.

5 Assessing reading comprehension

5.1 Introduction

When we assess reading comprehension, it should be to check that our pupils are reading texts they can understand. If texts are too difficult, what message are we sending? Children will learn to hate reading. It is not good for younger children to read difficult text above their reading capabilities. The best way for children to improve their comprehension is for them to read, but we should not make this hard for them by asking them to read difficult text. Some will say that unless they read hard text, they will not learn anything new, but the reality is that if the text is too hard, they will not learn anyway. The thing is that even in easier texts children can read, these texts do have new vocabulary and ideas that they can learn about and in that way incrementally build knowledge needed to comprehend better. Reading easier text and lots of it will help them gradually to build wide knowledge and vocabulary. Reading should be engaging and entertaining and educational and not so complex that the child has no idea what the text is all about.

This is the real purpose of assessment, not to find fault with children's comprehension but to make sure we are not condemning them to read books that are too difficult for them. It is to help them build their vocabulary and general knowledge while reading books they do understand. We need to make sure they are learning but not drowning in a sea of words.

This chapter will cover

- Assessing reading comprehension
- Standardised assessment
- Informal assessment
- Assessing background knowledge
- Assessing critical literacy skills

5.2 Assessing reading comprehension

The teacher gives a comprehension test, and the child reads passages that get more and more difficult. The teachers find that they cannot explain what the text is about even though they have just read it. Why is this? The obvious reason is

DOI: 10.4324/9781003130758-7

that the text is too difficult. If the text was easier, the student would be able to understand it.

The reason for assessment is to make sure children are engaging with text and enjoying and understanding what they read. We should not give young children texts to read that they will struggle to understand (Carver, 1987) even if they can decode the words in those texts. What is the point of being able to read the words if they do not understand the content?

It is poor teaching to give children difficult text to read. It especially does not make sense for younger readers. For older readers, yes, there may be times when they may to read certain texts that are too difficult, e.g., compulsory novels for English exams – but giving difficult texts to children still learning to read is unproductive and negative. Young children should read easier texts that they can understand.

Teachers know that the best way to build background knowledge is to read books but the problem is that many beginners cannot decode the words. The teacher can get around this by providing audio versions of content-rich books as long as the books are at their understanding level. This will enable beginner readers, and older less-skilled readers, to build their general knowledge and vocabulary. We all know children with decoding issues (e.g., dyslexia) who have good language and general knowledge, partly because they have access to audio books. They may not be able to read *Harry Potter*, but they can listen to it.

It is so important to assess comprehension, not to find out how poorly children are reading but to find out if what they are reading is comprehensible to them. Many passages in published teaching materials are impenetrable or vague or incoherent. Many of the books children have to read in school are too hard. Children cannot properly understand them. When we assess their comprehension, even if it is informal assessment, such as asking children for feedback about the setting, plot, and characters in a story, it will soon become evident if children are not understanding. This is a major value of comprehension assessment, to monitor children's learning and avoid making reading too hard.

Children need to read books that are well written, by good writers. This does not rule out decodable books. Many classic decodable books are well written, e.g., Dr Seuss' *Green Eggs and Ham* and so are modern decodable books, e.g., Sunshine Phonics Decodables series and Little Learners Love Literacy. On the other side of the coin, some books and magazine-type reading material for children seem more for adults than children; they are too clever, or too deep; they lose the children they are supposedly written for.

When children read books, we want them to "see" texts in an insightful way, as a coherent structure, just as an architect can see the framework of a house, can see in a deeper way than the average person who looks at the house from the street. Children can do this as well, read books like an architect "reads" a house. We can teach them to go beyond the surface words in the text, to see its deep structure. Then they will be better equipped to talk about and discuss the text. They will be comprehending it more fully.

5.3   Standardised assessment

A standardised measure is the best way to assess reading comprehension. It will immediately tell the teacher when the text is too difficult for the students they teach. They may be reading below their peers, but this is not an aspersion on the student. It is a signal that the text is too difficult. It then challenges the teacher to take action to find text material that the student can understand and gain knowledge from.

Giving children just one standardised test of reading comprehension can give insight, however some studies say that the teacher needs to use several such measures to gain a more comprehensive description of various aspects of student comprehension. Children sometimes achieve differently depending on the assessments used, such as multiple-choice questions versus open-ended questions (Calet et al., 2020).

A challenge for the teacher who does want to use a standardised test is that many standardised tests of reading comprehension require special training in assessment to access them from the publisher. One option is that if the school has its own assessment measures, and collects data for the whole school, then the teacher can access these data. If a standardised measure is available at your school, then of course use it, but the reality may be that it is not possible for the ordinary classroom teacher. The classroom teacher may have to use informal assessment methods.

5.4   Informal assessment

An informal way to assess comprehension is to talk about the text with pupils. Younger children are still developing their decoding skills so the best idea is to read them a book they can understand and then discuss the content material and any vocabulary that may not be familiar. For example, the story may have the word "socks." To the adult, "socks" seems a simple word but explaining its meaning may not be so simple for pupils, e.g., the teacher might say

T	– In the story, what are socks?
Children	– (no reply from the class)
T	– They are covers we put on our feet.
T	– In the story, what is the meaning of "catapulted"?
Children	– Jumped
T	– Good, maybe "flung out".

Teaching children the meanings of unknown words is part of teaching reading comprehension. It gives insight into the vocabulary knowledge of pupils. One quick way to teach an unfamiliar word to children is to suggest a synonym, e.g., a "sarcophagus" is a kind of coffin made of stone. For a word like "penguin," perhaps add something about its defining features, e.g., a "penguin" is a bird that can swim but is unable to fly.

5.5   Assessing background knowledge

If a text is too difficult for children to understand, the reason may be that they do not have the necessary background knowledge to comprehend. We know that background knowledge will vary considerably within the classroom. Studies have found large differences in vocabulary knowledge among school beginners from different social backgrounds (Hart & Risley, 1995).

Background knowledge is crucial in reading comprehension. If the teacher is talking about "weddings," yet the child has never been to a wedding and has little understanding of what one is – comprehension will be at risk. Alternatively, if the teacher is talking about "toasting the bride and groom" yet the only meaning the child associates with "toast" is the toast they had for breakfast (rather than part of a wedding celebration), then comprehension is at risk. Does the student have the necessary background knowledge to comprehend the teacher's meaning?

Authors such as Hirsch (2003, 2006, 2016) and Wexler (2019) have argued that children must have sufficient relevant background knowledge to understand their texts. When comprehension is hard for them, it is probably because they do not know enough about the topic. Wexler argued that comprehension is only as good as the student's general knowledge of the arts, civics, history, geography, science, maths – and other important subjects.

With younger children, if the texts they read or listen to are too hard to comprehend, we have to ask why we are asking them to listen to or read books that are so hard. Surely if the books they have to read in the early years of school are too hard for them to understand, then change the books so they read texts that they can understand. They may not know all the words or all the ideas (we can teach those), but they should be reading books where they know enough to understand reasonably well.

Lots of reading practice using texts beginner readers can decode and understand, e.g., decodable books, can build general knowledge and vocabulary. New words and ideas will come up in those texts. Given our awareness of the importance of background knowledge and how critical it is for comprehension, rather than push too hard, it would be better to give beginners material to read that is within their knowledge.

5.6   Assessing critical literacy

Do children in the class have critical literacy skills? Are they showing evidence of critical literacy when they have an opinion, ask questions of the author, go beyond the text, ask about the authenticity of the content, and double-check the facts? Are we teaching these skills?

Critical literacy is particularly important for the 21st century. How often are we bombarded with "facts" and how do we determine if the information is fact or fiction? Critical thinking involves problem solving, the ability to communicate effectively in reading and writing. A person showing critical literacy, according to the Greeks, "was someone who could explain and judge the merits and shortcomings of an event or object" (Calfee & Patrick, 1995, p. 73). Furthermore, "critical literacy entails ... the capacity to think analytically, to gain insights, and ... to communicate with others about it in speech and in writing" (p. 73).

Basic literacy is being able to read the cereal package, but critical literacy is being able to discern whether the ingredients are, in fact, healthy or not. Critical questions require students to form an opinion or judgement about the text. The answers are not right or wrong, rather critical questions encourage students to challenge the texts they read or listen to.

Assessing critical literacy will add to the teacher's multi-faceted analysis of children's comprehension skills. To build critical literacy skills in story comprehension, teachers need for children to go beyond the text, to ask out of the square questions, such as

- Could the story be set elsewhere?
- What would a different ending be?
- Could the author include other characters?
- Who/what would they be?
- Are there gaps in this story?
- Do you think the author could include more information?

5.7   Conclusion

The value of assessing reading comprehension is that it can help teachers to know where their class is at, what kinds of material the class can properly understand, and to give the teacher direction in finding books that are more suitable for their pupils. The most accurate way of assessing reading comprehension is to use a combination of standardised and informal assessments. If teachers know what reading level their pupils are at, then they will be able to monitor the books they read to ensure that they are not too difficult. Unfortunately, much published material is not at the right level, and often is it the developing reader who is stuck with text that is too hard to read. That has to be soul-destroying; they will turn away from books, thinking they are "dumb."

The teacher who ruthlessly checks the difficulty of text that is supposed to be appropriate for their class against their own actual data for each pupil from classroom assessments, is in a much better position to ensure that their pupils are reading books and other texts that they can understand - and that they can discuss effectively with the teacher. We want children to read books they can enjoy and comprehend easily because we want them to be sophisticated consumers of text, to learn new words, to seek out new knowledge, to learn how writers write and the structures they use. There is no way we can take them to these new destinations if they have to read books that are impenetrable to them. This is where data gathered from comprehension assessment can help. It enables the teacher to gain feedback about how well their pupils are learning and how effectively they are teaching.

6 Teaching reading comprehension

6.1 Introduction

Teaching about text structure helps children to comprehend text information in an organised way. It develops a range of thinking skills. They learn to be critical thinkers, to ask insightful questions, and to analyse strengths and weaknesses in the design of the content they learn in class. Reading comprehension becomes more than reading the words, or retelling the text; it is about thinking like a writer, knowing why the writer wrote those words, the "what and why" of their text message.

Young children in the first years of school acquire a more formal language for talking about text, that is, the "academic" language used by teachers. Children enter school with their own natural language but school has a different way of talking about texts. When teachers talk to each other about text structure, they use this academic language and we need to encourage students to do the same. We have found that children do like learning academic vocabulary, technical words like "narrative," "characters," and "plot."

Text structure knowledge helps with comprehension because the reader has to re-create the way the writer constructed the content, to "see" the meaning in a more organised way. The reader can pinpoint any "gaps" that are in the text, i.e., missing content knowledge that they as readers are expected to bring to the text to make sense of it. The text structure approach can simplify the sea of detail and make the text more comprehensible.

Even when reading the simplest of texts, talking about text structure helps children to stand back from the story or topic, look for the big picture, learn how writers think, how they designed the text to make it interesting. When children use these skills, they ask themselves "big picture" questions – What am I doing? Why am I doing it? What will I learn from it?

This chapter covers the following topics:

- Developmental guide for teaching story structure
- Story webs
- Story graphs
- Example of a story web
- Expository text – the list

DOI: 10.4324/9781003130758-8

- Expository text – the text web
- Expository text – the text weave
- Expository text – the linear string
- Expository text – the repetitive cycle

6.2   Developmental guide for teaching story structure

The teacher does not have to teach everything about story structure all at once. It is better to simplify, to teach just some aspects of story structure in the beginning stages, and to build up more detail as children become more familiar with the elements of story.

Calfee and Patrick (1995, p. 171) suggested a developmental guide for teaching young children about the elements of a story – see Table 6.1. For younger children the web can focus on the basic aspects of the story without too much detail.

For older students the story web can bring in more sophisticated ideas such as the mood of the setting, character motives, a more detailed analysis of the different episodes in the story, and how the theme of the story relates to the why of the plot, why the characters did what they did, and the consequences of their actions.

Table 6.1 Developmental Stages in Analysing a Story.

	Age 5	*Age 6*	*Age 7*	*Age 8*
Characters	Identify major and minor – describe traits	Compare and contrast characters by describing their traits	Create new characters	Describe character motives and feelings
Setting	Where, When	Mood	Create new settings	
Plot	Identify events	Analyse episodes	Summarise	
Theme	Identify lesson learned	Describe how the story affects the reader as a person	Link to moral values	Describe how theme is shaped by characters and plot

6.3   Teaching the structure of narrative text

Teachers read stories to their class most days. This is a great opportunity to look at their text structure. Students already have an intuitive idea of "story" that they have learned from watching television, and listening to stories at home. Life is a story. What they do not know, in a formal sense, is the technical structure of stories, how they are built. This is where the teacher can help students, to look inside a story to see how it works.

Children need to talk formally about the text structure of the story, its design, and use the academic vocabulary of writers, e.g., the setting, the main characters, the problem-solution nature of the plot, and the overall message or theme of the story. Talking about text structure and using the technical terms of writing gives the class the language tools they need to comprehend the content more clearly, see it in a simpler way, and it will help them better to express their ideas about the story:

1. Setting. The teacher can explain the features of a story setting that shows when and where the story takes place. Various details in the story can help to reveal the time and place, e.g., the way characters are dressed, the age of buildings, and form of transport.
2. Character/s. The class can list the major and minor characters and compare them in dress, personality, behaviour.
3. Plot. The teacher can explain how the plot works. The plot describes the action in the story. The plot shows the first thing that happened, the second thing, and so on. For beginners, a simple way to show the plot is to draw a time line or story graph – see Figure 6.1. The story graph shows two aspects of the plot, the level of emotion or action (high, middle, low) and the time sequence of action (event 1, event 2, etc.) For older children, another way to deconstruct the plot is to describe each episode. A story can have one or more episodes. An episode has four parts – problem, response, action, and outcome – see Figure 6.2.
4. Theme. The theme is the message of the story. Some children may not know the meaning of the word theme so perhaps use synonyms such as message, lesson learned, or "moral" of the story. An example of theme might be a story where the character has something nice for a while but then has to give it back, which suggests a theme of "Enjoy things while you have them."

Story web

A story structure is like a spider web where each part connects with the other – see Figure 6.2. The web is a simple graphic design to show children the four main parts of a story – setting, characters, plot, and theme.

- Setting – stories take place somewhere at a particular time, e.g., "At such a time I found out for certain that this bleak place overgrown with nettles …"
- Characters – have features (hair, eyes, clothing), personality (happy, sad, grumpy) and can be compared with each other (similarities and differences)
- Plot – consists of one or more episodes – each episode starts with a challenge/problem, then a response to the problem, action to do something about the problem, and a solution or outcome. Stories may have more than one episode. Some episodes may have a complication to solving the problem that has to be resolved somehow.
- Theme – the message intended for the reader. The theme is not always explicitly stated. Stories may have more than one theme/message.

When teaching the class about story structure, one idea is to use a modelling book to diagram the ideas in the story. A modelling book is an enlarged notebook, large enough for the class to see what the teacher writes down on the blank pages.

The lesson might start with a focus on character. The teacher might divide the page in half and write ideas that compare the two main characters. The teacher is making a character "weave." Then on another page, the teacher draws up a story "web." In the story web, there is information about setting (when, where), a list of characters (major, minor), the plot (problem-response-action-outcome), and the theme or message of the story. It means the teacher has a written record to keep for the future. Students can go back to it to look at examples of work they have done on story webs.

Story graph

A story graph is another way to teach story structure. Longer stories divide into episodes but simpler stories might best be captured in a story graph – see Figure 6.1. A story graph shows visually the level of action (low to high), and level of emotion/ feelings (low to high). In this approach, the teacher asks students to recall events of the story. Then, the teacher places these on the story graph in order of events. When placing the events on the story graph, children need to decide whether the event is low action or high action. After placing the events on the graph, the class connects the events by drawing a time line.

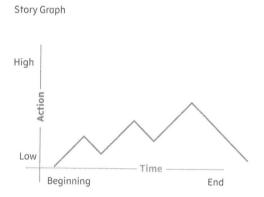

Figure 6.1 Story Graph – Time Line and Level of Action/emotion

Lesson plan for Edward the Emu

The following lesson plan shows how to use the story web approach (Dymock & Nicholson, 2010) to tackle the children's book, *Edward the Emu* (Knowles, 1988). The teacher could use the story with very young children but will have to read it to them. With older children they may be able to read along or read it for themselves.

The story is about an emu at an Australian zoo. It is the classic theme of "the grass looks greener on the other side." Edward was not happy with zoo life, was very bored, and thought the other animals in the zoo were better off. Edward left the emu enclosure and tried living alongside other animals in their enclosures, like the seal, lion, and snake. Edward found out, though, that each animal had its own challenges. In the end, Edward goes back to the emu piece of space in the zoo. Edward realized that being an emu was better for him. The theme was that it is better to be your own self than to wish you were like others who seem better off.

The lesson plan below can be used flexibly depending on time available and the reading level of the class. It could focus on one component of a story, such as setting, characters, plot, theme – or more than one. It would depend on student knowledge. For very young children, it may be better to start with characters and setting. Then later, move to the plot, and finally the theme. The following lesson plan focuses on all the components of this narrative but it is OK to select just one to focus on.

The teacher might ask background questions like

T: Who can tell me what a zoo is?

T: What sort of animals do you think we would find at the zoo?

T: I have some pictures of animals. Which ones might we find at the zoo? [Teacher shows the class pictures of various animals, e.g., pets such as cats and dogs; farm animals such as cows and sheep; animals one might find at the zoo such as giraffes, tigers, lions].

T: Let us group them into two groups: zoo animals and animals you would not find in the zoo.

T: Today we are reading the story, *Edward the Emu*. The author is Sheena Knowles.

T: Who can tell me what an emu is? Here is a picture of an emu (show cover or page from the book). Close your eyes and try to picture an emu in your head. Can you picture an emu?

T: Stories have important elements/parts. Can you remember what these parts are? (characters, setting, plot and theme).

T: As I read the first few pages, I want you to think about who the main character is. How would you describe the main character? I'll read what the author wrote: "Edward the emu was sick of the zoo. There was nowhere to go, there was nothing to do. And compared to the seals that lived right next door, well, being an emu was frankly a bore."

T: Who do you think the main character is? Yes, Edward the emu. The title of the book does give us a clue, doesn't it?

T: As I read the story, I want you to think about Edward. What is Edward like in personality? What does Edward look like?

  • Features – Large bird, feathers, beak, little wings, red eye, long neck, two legs, large claws, blue and black head.
  • Personality – Bored, not happy being an emu, tried to be a seal, lion, snake.

T: Let's think about the setting. Where does the story take place? When does it take place?

T: What is the plot?

- Problem: Edward was "sick of the zoo" and bored being an emu
- Response: Bored, sad
- Action: Edward decided to become a different animal as it seemed the seal, lion and snake were better off
- Outcome: Eventually Edward realised that being an emu was best. Edward returns to the emu enclosure where he meets Edwina (another emu). Edward is happy being "Edward" again.

T: What is the theme: Possible theme was "Be happy with who you are."
T: Now let us draw a visual diagram of the story. We are using a story web structure. The information to go into the web will be –

Characters – Edward and Edwina
Setting – The zoo is "where" and present day is "when"
Plot – the episode structure is

- Problem (no excitement)
- Response (not happy)
- Action (joins other animals)
- Outcome (realizes his life is not so bad)

Theme of story – you can be happy with who you are

T: Now, together we can use the information in our diagram to write a summary of *Edward the Emu* – see Figure 6.2.

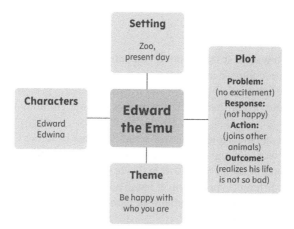

Figure 6.2 Story Web Structure for Edward the Emu

6.4   Teaching expository text structure

Expository texts are different and often more challenging than narrative texts. They are not stories. They convey information about people, events, and things in the world. They can have a descriptive or a sequential structure. One reason they are more challenging is that there are a number of different expository text structures. In addition, the vocabulary in these texts is often more technical and unfamiliar to children than in stories.

There are three main descriptive texts that five-to-eight-year-old readers encounter. They are the list pattern, web pattern, and compare-contrast (weave) patterns. We have encountered these text types countless times in early years reading material.

List

This is where there is a listing of the attributes of something. It is rather like a shopping list. It does not matter what comes first in the list. An example of a list structure is the decodable book, *Markets* (George, 2022a), written at a six-year-level. There is a list of goods that can be purchased at markets (e.g., "You can shop for carpets and hats … dishes and bags" [pp. 9–10]). There is a list of food to purchase at markets (e.g., "There is farm food at the market" [p. 13]).

Web

The web structure is about one thing, e.g., birds, butterflies, and wombats, the city of Sydney. A web structure has one main topic and a number of subtopics, e.g., for a wombat, it might be appearance, habitat, and diet.

Weave

A weave is like a web in structure but it compares more than one thing. Texts with a weave structure compare and contrast two or more things, e.g., butterflies and moths; kangaroos and wallabies; bees and wasps; different kinds of dinosaurs (e.g., tyrannosaurus and brontosaurus). The weave is another common descriptive text structure.

The weave is an extension of the web structure. That is, rather than focusing on one thing – the weave compares and contrasts two or more things, e.g., the children's instructional reader *From Here to There* (George, 2022b), at a seven-year-level, compares different types of travel but in a light-hearted way. In Table 6.2, the weave summarises the reasons (sometimes humorous) given in the text as to why we use different kinds of transport.

Table 6.2 Weave Structure for "From Here to There."

Form of transport	Why we use it
Jet	Quick form of travel
High-speed train	If in a rush
Paddling	If not in a rush
Canal Boat	If you have canals
Bike	Travel to town
Camel	Sit up high
Wheelchair	Unable to walk
Scooter	Fun

Linear string

Some texts describe a procedure, where there are a series of steps, such as a recipe on how to make fish pie, or the steps involved in making coffee. It is like a flowchart structure. For example, we found a linear string structure in an article for children about the steps in "making a road." It was written at the eight-year-level and showed the steps that builders have to go through, from consulting the public, to finishing off the road with traffic lights and painting in lane markings – see Figure 6.3.

Sequence - Making a road

Figure 6.3 Linear String Structure for "Making a Road"

Cyclical

Older children will come across texts that describe a cyclical sequence such as the life cycle of a cicada (eggs, nymphs, adults) where the cycle repeats itself. A simpler example of a cyclical structure for younger children might be the seasons (summer, autumn, winter, spring) – Figure 6.4.

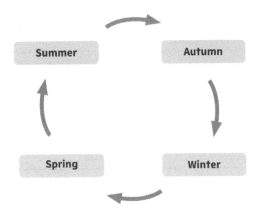

Figure 6.4 Cyclical Sequence for Seasons of the year

6.5   Conclusion

Learning about text structure is interesting and fun and it is a key to comprehension. To be able to "see" texts in an organised way, to see the framework of text, its structure, helps the reader to store its meaning more easily in memory. Teaching text structure shows children the elements of text design, about how writers structure their writing to maximum effect. Understanding structure helps to de-mystify texts. It shows children how effective writing does not just come out of the blue, but it follows a careful structure, that effective writers use structure.

Part III

Reading Vocabulary

7 Vocabulary

What is it?

7.1 Introduction

Vocabulary knowledge is word knowledge. It is a person's knowledge of the body of words in a particular language. There are many words in the English language, more than half a million. Then there are all the words we know that are not in the dictionary, people's names, names of songs, soccer teams, supermarket products, and so on. There are so many words. It is easy to take vocabulary for granted but it means a lot. Its importance becomes immediately apparent for a tourist visiting a country where they do not speak the language.

Until the 1980s, research on the nature of vocabulary was so limited that Calfee and Drum (1978) wrote of vocabulary research as a "vanishing species" (p. 217). At that time, researchers focused on vocabulary size and quality of vocabulary, particularly the difference between productive and receptive vocabulary. This has changed. For example, in the last decade, the internet search engine Pro-Quest shows a huge increase in vocabulary research, and there are now hundreds of articles coming out each year.

This chapter covers

- What does it mean to "know" a word?
- How many words do children need to know to read well?
- The reciprocal relation of vocabulary and reading
- The importance of reading for learning new vocabulary – an example

7.2   What does it mean to "know" a word?

The dictionary (Merriam-Webster, n.d.) defines *word* as "A speech sound or series of speech sounds that symbolizes and communicates a meaning usually without being divisible into smaller units capable of independent use."

What do we mean when we say we "know a word"? It probably means we recognise the word and can explain what it means but there is much more to understanding a word than this. Consider your understanding of the following Anglo-Saxon words: *pencil*, *date*, *point*, and *needle*. How well would a five-to-seven-year-old student know these words? Would they be able to define the four words?

DOI: 10.4324/9781003130758-10

What does it mean to know a word well? Calfee and Drum (1986, pp. 825–826) wrote that knowing a word well involved "depth of meaning; precise usage; facile access; the ability to articulate one's understanding; flexibility in the application of the knowledge of a word; the appreciation of metaphor, analogy, word play; the ability to recognise a synonym, to define, to use a word expressively."

How long does it take to know a word well? This is a difficult question to answer. The pathway to knowing a word is incremental. There are stages in knowing a word. Given there are over 600,000 words in English (see the Oxford English Dictionary website – https://www.oed.com/), it is very likely that there are many words we know well and words we do not know. Dale and O'Rourke (1986) suggested there were four stages of word knowledge:

Stage 1: Never saw/heard it before
Stage 2: Heard it but don't know what it means
Stage 3: Recognise it in context as having something to do with …
Stage 4: Know the word well

Let's return to the four words: *pencil*, *date*, *point*, and *needle*. What stage would five-to-seven-year-old children be at with each word? While there are no data on how well five-year-old students know the four words, we have taken an educated guess at their possible word knowledge. Table 7.1 suggests that five-year-old students could be at Stage 1 with the words *point* and *needle*, Stage 3 with the word *date*, and Stage 4 with the word *pencil*.

Table 7.1 Five-Year-Old Students' (Suggested) Knowledge of the Words "Pencil, Date, Point, Needle."

Word	Stage 1	Stage 2	Stage 3	Stage 4
Pencil				X
Date			X	
Point	X			
Needle	X			

Table 7.2 suggests that seven-year-old students are at Stage 2, 3, or 4 in their understanding of the words *pencil*, *date*, *point*, and *needle*. It is likely that students will progress in their knowledge of the four words, over time.

Table 7.2 Seven-Year-Old Students' (Suggested) Knowledge of the Words "Pencil, Date, Point, Needle."

Word	Stage 1	Stage 2	Stage 3	Stage 4
Pencil				X
Date				*X*
Point			X	
Needle		X		

Five-year-old students would normally have an understanding of the word *pencil* as they use a pencil to draw and write. Five-to-seven-year-old students might be at Stage 4 with the word *pencil* although it has more than one meaning (e.g., pencil the meeting, pencil to write with).

Five-to-seven-year-old students will most likely have an understanding of at least one definition of the word *date* (e.g., today's date) but they may not be aware that the word *date* also has multiple meanings (e.g., we can date someone, we can eat dates). If this is the case, students would likely be at Stage 3 (or 4).

Students in their first year at school may not know one of the meanings of *point* and it is very unlikely they will know that the word *point* has more than 30 different meanings. While a six-to-seven-year-old student may know "not to *point*" [at someone] or that their "soccer team scored three *points*" they are unlikely to know the many different meanings of the word *point*.

Needle is another word that five-year-old students may not have heard so they would be at Stage 1. Slightly older students may have some understanding of the word *needle* but their understanding is most likely not well developed (c.g., we can needle someone in sport; nurses use a needle for injections; knitting needle, sewing needle).

Cronbach (1942) identified five categories or dimensions of word knowledge. The categories are as follows:

1 Generalisation – able to define the word
2 Application – able to use the word correctly
3 Breadth – knows multiple meanings of a word
4 Precision – knows when and when not to use a word
5 Availability – able to use the word productively

One of the strengths of Cronbach's dimensions is the *breadth* category. That is, knowing that many words have multiple meanings.

Let's look at the Anglo-Saxon word *park*. Three of the meanings below do resemble one another (i.e., park the car; park a bag, car gears in "park") but the word *park* can also mean a large grassy area, often with trees and shrubs.

1 Sarah went to the local park with her family.
2 John had to park his car on a hill.
3 Please park your bag by the chair.
4 Is your car in park?

What does it mean to know the word *park*? It means having an understanding of its core meaning but also knowing that context plays a role. Context, in the examples above, helps us define *park*.

Consider the Anglo-Saxon word *bank*. *Bank* can either be a noun or a verb. Can this word be defined if it is out of context? How would you define the word *bank*?

If a student asked you what "bank" meant which definition would you provide? A precise definition would depend on the context.

1   Our local bank is closing.
2   The pilot banked the plane.
3   I sat on the river bank.

It takes many encounters with a word before Stage 4 is reached. There are variations between researchers on how many encounters are necessary before a word is known well.

Saragi et al. (1978) found that native speakers of English needed to encounter target words at least ten times before substantial learning occurred. Nation (2020) argued the need for many repetitions and practice to learn words that there are at least nine different aspects to knowing the meaning of a word.

McKeown et al. (1985) suggested that after 12 encounters with a word, reading comprehension improves but while reading comprehension improves, it does not mean the word is known well. Nagy and Scott (2000) suggested that it is after 40 encounters with a word that it is known well. Word knowledge is not just about producing a dictionary definition. It is much more than this.

7.3   How many words do children need to know to read well?

Learning vocabulary is an enormous task. We begin life with a vocabulary of zero, and over the years, we learn the meaning of thousands of words. On school entry, however, there is a significant gap in vocabulary knowledge between children from different walks of life. Hart and Risley (1995) spent an hour each month for 2.5 years with a group of young children recording everything that was spoken by the child and around the child, from the age of seven-to-nine months to three years. They recorded and transcribed over 1318 hour-long observations. The 42 families in the study were from upper, middle, and lower socioeconomic (SES) backgrounds. They found by the age of three years; there was a huge vocabulary gap between language spoken in high and low SES families. That is, some children had heard 30 million words more than their counter parts. They described this gap as "the early catastrophe" (Hart & Risley, 2003, p. 4).

Biemiller and Slonim (2001) found that Grade 2 children (aged 7–8 years) in the lowest quartile had vocabularies similar to the average child in kindergarten (five to six years old). Some children are commencing school with a less than optimal vocabulary and the risk is they will learn new vocabulary at a rate less than those commencing school with a higher vocabulary. Consider the implications for the classroom teacher given that some children will have much larger vocabularies than their counter parts. It is critical that teachers help these children learn vocabulary at an accelerated rate.

Does it matter that some children, on school entry, have had many more encounters with words, compared with their classmates? Yes, it does. Walker et al. (1994)

tracked 32 children from Hart and Risley's (1995) study, from three years of age to the end of third grade. They found that the gap in vocabulary knowledge as those students progressed through school magnified.

Hart and Risley's (1995) research indicated that on school entry, there was huge variance in student vocabulary knowledge. Estimates are that on school entry the gap in vocabulary size among students in the classroom could be between 2500 and 5000 or more words. Researchers vary in their estimates, however.

Children's vocabulary knowledge increases, on average, by about 3000–4000 word families each year (Graves, 2006). A word family is a group of words that have the same root or base. Word families for the Anglo-Saxon words *look, happy,* and *help* would be *looked, looking, look, looks*; *happiness, happier, unhappy*; and *helper, helping, unhelpful, helpful, helpless, helped*. Word pairs such as *home* and *homely* or *fall and infallible* are not part of the same word family, as they do not have the same core meaning (Duff & Brydon, 2020).

7.4 The reciprocal relation of vocabulary and reading

Nagy (2005) argued that the relationship between vocabulary and reading comprehension goes in both directions – see Figure 7.1. A large vocabulary contributes positively to reading comprehension and strengths in comprehension contribute positively learning new vocabulary.

Reading comprehension is a multicomponent process involving strengths in word recognition skills and linguistic comprehension. Vocabulary knowledge is a subcomponent of linguistic comprehension and is a predictor of reading comprehension progress (Hjetland et al., 2017, 2019).

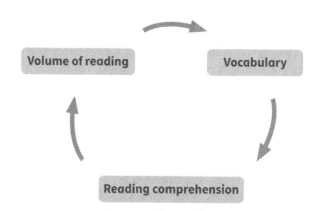

Figure 7.1 Reciprocal Relationship of Vocabulary and Reading Comprehension

Hirsch (2003, 2016) wrote of the important role of vocabulary knowledge in reading comprehension. It makes common sense. If you do not know what the words in the text mean, comprehension is at serious risk. For example, in a well-known study (Marks et al., 1974), the researchers replaced a small number of low-frequency words in the text with higher frequency words. Children's reading comprehension increased significantly as a result.

Have you visited a country where you don't speak the language? If the Italian speaker (or the text) used the word "biciletta" would you know what it means? Would it cut you out of the conversation? If you knew "biciletta" meant "bike," then you would have *some* understanding of the topic.

Vocabulary and general knowledge play a significant role in reading comprehension. Students with a large vocabulary are at an advantage in terms of comprehension. Students with a large vocabulary on a given topic (e.g., kangaroos) will understand better an article about kangaroos. Students with a large vocabulary about volcanoes are advantaged when being read to or reading about volcanoes. What's more – as they read about animals or volcanoes, they are likely to learn more content-specific vocabulary than students who do not know a lot about animals or volcanoes.

Mancilla-Martinez and McClain (2020) found that students who understand the vocabulary of a topic were more likely to:

- Learn new words about that topic
- Comprehend the topic
- Productively use words about that topic
- Develop a more conceptual understanding

This "rich-get-richer, poor get poorer" effect of having a rich depth of vocabulary knowledge was explained in a classic article by Stanovich (1986). An early advantage in vocabulary knowledge and reading progress leads to further advantages in vocabulary and reading comprehension.

Children who have a rich vocabulary are better at reading comprehension. This leads them to read more, which then contributes to further gains in vocabulary and reading comprehension. Children with impoverished vocabularies have lower levels of reading comprehension. They do not understand the text as well, and they read less. This leads to less growth in vocabulary and reading comprehension. That is, the "poor get poorer."

Does the reader need to know all the words being read (or listened to) to comprehend? Nagy and Scott (2000) estimated between 90 and 95% of words need to be known to the reader for adequate comprehension. If the reader knows 90–95% of the words, they can use this knowledge to learn the balance of unknown words. If more than 10% of the words are unknown, then comprehension is at serious risk, as is the opportunity to learn new vocabulary.

Thus, if the text has too many unknown words, the reader can use context clues to unlock the meaning of some of them but not all of them. Pressley (2000) wrote that "if a word is not known to the reader, then the reader's understanding of it depends entirely on context clues" but unfortunately "readers often do not infer correctly the meaning of a word from context clues" (p. 548).

Up until the age of school entry vocabulary is learnt through exposure to oral language and listening to books being read. The Hart and Risley (1995) study suggested that a considerable amount of oral language was critical for vocabulary growth in young children. The contribution of oral language and print exposure to vocabulary growth continues into the early years of schooling as students begin to develop the skill of decoding, which will in time give them access to texts, to read on their own. A rich oral language environment and listening to books being read by the teacher (e.g., picture books, big books, and appropriate novels) is critical for vocabulary growth in the first few years of school.

7.5 The importance of reading as a way to learn vocabulary – an example

To illustrate this, let us turn to an extract from *Possum Magic* (Fox, 1983), written for younger students. In the book, the author wrote,

> They ate ANZAC biscuits in Adelaide, mornay and Minties in Melbourne, steak and salad in Sydney and pumpkin scones in Brisbane. Hush remained invisible. "Don't lose heart!" said Grandma Poss. "Let's see what we can find in Darwin."

A five-year-old may not have a measurable understanding of, or know in any deep way, the meaning of the words, *ANZAC, mornay, Minties, remained, invisible,* nor the meaning of the phrase "don't lose heart." They may not be familiar with Australian cities mentioned in the book (e.g., Adelaide, Melbourne, Sydney, Brisbane, or Darwin) but children will not learn these words, phrases or develop an understanding of the cities without some exposure to them. After multiple exposures to ANZAC biscuit and perhaps eating an ANZAC biscuit, students will likely gain an understanding of the word. Over time, after many exposures, and an explanation of what ANZAC represents, children will develop a deeper understanding. Learning the meaning of words is a slow process. A key to vocabulary development is exposure to text.

7.6 Conclusion

There are many words children simply do not know the meaning of – or have never heard before. Teachers can help students to learn new vocabulary by raising children's awareness of words. Luckily, children are "little linguists" and will learn many new words if they read a lot and if we teach them about words. In any one text, there may be some new words they do not know, and it pays to explain them and learn them.

Teaching about words encourages a love of words and an interest in words. It encourages students to become passionate about words, so that when they see a new word, they will try to work out what it means, and will reach for the dictionary when not sure, and when they write, they will think about the "best" word to use. They will like words.

8 Assessing vocabulary

8.1 Introduction

How does a teacher of five-to-eight-year-old children assess vocabulary? Does the teacher measure receptive vocabulary (words we hear or receive through reading and listening) or productive vocabulary (words we produce in oral language and in writing)? The results would be quite different, at any age, and particularly in the early years of school. Research has shown that our receptive vocabulary is larger than our productive vocabulary. We understand more words than we produce through speech or writing.

This chapter covers

- Standardised assessment of vocabulary
- Informal assessment through retelling
- Informal assessment through teacher observation
- Informal assessment with questionnaires

8.2 Standardised measures

Children's receptive vocabulary is larger than their productive vocabulary (Segbers & Schroeder, 2017). Standardised assessment measures such as the *Picture Peabody Vocabulary Test* (PPVT-5, Dunn, 2018) or the UK version, the *British Picture Vocabulary Scale*, are accurate ways of assessing children's receptive vocabulary knowledge. However, these tests and others like them are not readily available in schools and training in how to administer standardised assessments is necessary before teachers can purchase the tests, so using these measures is not an easy option for most teachers of young children unless they sign up for training or know someone who has done the training.

A more feasible option is for the school to organise the purchase and administration of more readily available measures such as the *Progressive Achievement Tests* (PAT), especially the PAT *Vocabulary* assessment measure (see Australian Council for Educational research [ACER] website, https://www.acer.org/au/pat). This test, according to ACER's website, measures vocabulary knowledge in "knowing, applying, categorising, and morphology." In addition, the website states the test

DOI: 10.4324/9781003130758-11

assesses students' ability to identify the meaning of words, put words into categories, and identify the meaning of roots and affixes. The test is available for students aged 7 years and beyond. It is important, however, for teachers to be aware that this measure is dependent upon students' decoding ability, as students are required to read the text of the test in order to complete the assessment. For children with decoding issues, we need to be aware that PAT *Vocabulary* results may not reflect their true vocabulary knowledge.

8.3   Informal vocabulary assessment

Retelling

Retelling a story is an informal measure of vocabulary and comprehension, although not recommended as the sole measure (Cao & Kim, 2021). Retellings have the advantage of being *natural*, but they have limitations as they rely on the productive language skills of the student (Stahl et al., 2019). Shy and less-verbal students may not do as well even though their receptive language skills might be very advanced.

According to Ralli et al. (2021, p. 951), "story retelling is a complicated process which involves a range of abilities." These abilities include both the ability to receive language and express language. Ralli et al. explained that for young learners (aged 4–6) vocabulary is a predictor of their ability to understand narratives, and retellings are correlated with both receptive and expressive vocabulary.

The following suggestions are for assessing vocabulary based on story retelling.

- Select several stories (e.g., picture books) that are preferably unknown to a small group of students.
- Ask the students to select one to be read aloud and discussed.
- While reading stop and discuss key ideas (e.g., characters, setting, aspects of the plot). Encourage discussion.
- Retell 1:1. Ask the student to retell the story. Make a note of the vocabulary used, particularly descriptive words and vocabulary that focuses on the character's feelings (e.g., scared, excited, sad). Consider the number of descriptive words used (limited vs. wide range) and the number of words that focus on the character's feelings (limited vs. wide range).

As an example, let us focus on the picture book, Edward the Emu, as it is known to many teachers though it is not a story we recommend using it to assess vocabulary knowledge as it is so well known. A suggested scoring of vocabulary used in a retelling of Edward the Emu could be – see Table 8.1.

An alternate story that the teacher could use to assess vocabulary, one that is suitable for five-to-eight-year-olds and that has several possibly unfamiliar words e.g., *tripod*, *gawking*, and *harmonica* is Farmer Palmer's Wagon Ride by William Steig.

Table 8.1 Assessing Vocabulary Based on Retelling – *Edward the Emu.*

Basic vocabulary	Between basic and developed	Developed vocabulary
Everyday content words, e.g., *Edward, seal, lion;* function words, e.g., *he*; verbs, e.g., *went*	Some descriptive words, e.g., *bored.*	A range of sophisticated and descriptive words, e.g., *grand, frankly, dissatisfied*

Teacher observation

Teacher observation, while not as accurate as standardised measures, is certainly helpful in determining vocabulary knowledge, e.g., the teacher taking notice of word choices that children use during classroom or 1:1 discussion. Some children do have amazing vocabulary. An example of this, in a humorous cartoon, showed a student telling a friend that they got detention for calling another pupil "obsequious." What puzzled the pupil was that the teacher also gave them a credit for it. Well, we know the teacher was definitely observing vocabulary knowledge in that class!

Questionnaire

The *Vocabulary Knowledge Scale* (VKS) (Brown, 2008) is where students indicate how well they know the selected vocabulary. This is particularly useful prior to teaching a unit in the content area (e.g., environment, science, social studies). It will give the teacher an insight into children's knowledge of upcoming words in the study unit.

The scale, over time, if used as a pretest and posttest, can measure gains in word knowledge, and provide an indication of key vocabulary associated with the unit being taught and whether children have learned the unfamiliar vocabulary.

Prior to teaching a study unit in the content area, the teacher selects key words students will encounter in the unit. Normally, children individually complete the assessment. For very young children, the assessment can be completed by the teacher either 1:1 or in small groups where the teacher reads each word aloud. Below is a modified version of VKS and the categories children need to select – see Tables 8.2 and 8.3.

Categories

A: I know what this word means and I can use it in a sentence.
B: I know what this word means, but I'm not sure how to use it.
C: I've seen/heard this word/phrase before, but I don't know what it means.
D: I've never seen/heard this word/phrase before.

Table 8.2 Vocabulary Knowledge Scale – Upcoming Study Unit on the Environment.

	A	B	C	D
Environment				
Pollution				
Climate				
Water quality				
Earth				
Plastics				

Table 8.3 Vocabulary Knowledge Scale – Study Unit on Wombats.

	A	B	C	D
Wombat				
Mammal				
Native animal				
Habitat				
Diet				
Enemies				

We trialled the VKS tool on one child for the study unit on wombats. Below are the VKS scores for her responses. All her responses were in Category A – "I know what this word means and I can use it in a sentence." The VKS for this child clearly shows she is unlikely to experience challenges comprehending a text/unit on wombats – see Table 8.4.

Table 8.4 Student Answers – Vocabulary Knowledge Scale – Study Unit on Wombats.

	A	B	C	D
Wombat	X			
Mammal	X			
Native animal	X			
Habitat	X			
Diet	X			
Enemies	X			

Her sentences were

Wombat: *Wombats are cute and fluffy and you find them in Australia.*
Mammal: *A dolphin is a mammal because they have live young and they feed their babies milk.*
Native: *The kiwi is a native bird to New Zealand. Kiwis aren't mammals.*

Habitat: *The beaver's natural habitat is in a dam and a lake.*
Diet: *I am on a special diet so I can't eat meat.*
Enemies: *A mouse's enemy is a cat and a cat's enemy is a dog.*

8.4   Conclusion

Assessing a child's vocabulary in the early years is an essential part of their academic and personal progress. There are standardised assessment measures teachers can use, but there are also informal ways to measure vocabulary depth and breadth. Teacher observation is possible when discussing books during reading time. Retellings of stories and articles, either orally or in writing, can give insights into children's growing academic vocabulary. Other informal measures to gauge vocabulary knowledge are questionnaires like the VKS. All these measures are important ways to track vocabulary growth. A rich and diverse vocabulary is a key to academic success.

9 Teaching vocabulary

9.1 Introduction

In the first five years of school, some studies suggest that children are likely to come across up to 80,000 different words (Juel & Minden-Cupp, 2003). It seems a massive challenge. How can children learn the meanings of so many words?

What should the teacher do? Teaching new vocabulary takes time and practice, and teachers can only teach a small number of new words effectively each day. Some schools have lists of "important" words that teachers are supposed to teach but they are only a drop in the ocean of words that children need to know to succeed in school.

One idea for the teacher is to look at the bigger picture, to find a better way. Achieving this huge vocabulary target will not happen overnight. It will take time and the reality is that children will need to be their own teachers and learn new words on their own, "in loco parentis," by reading as much as they can.

The teacher can continue to teach vocabulary but focus on words in an academic way, teach children technical terms to help them learn words for themselves, teach the structure of words, and teach how words relate to each other as synonyms, antonyms, and so on. Teach how many words have literal and figurative meanings, multiple meanings, how word meanings are part of the Story of English. The teacher can do all these things, can make words interesting to children, and inspire a love of words.

This chapter covers ways to teach vocabulary including:

- Use of context clues
- Use of concept maps
- Use of the dictionary and thesaurus
- Use of word analysis
- Encouraging reading "mileage"

9.2 Context clues help to learn new words

Sternberg (1987) wrote that most vocabulary is learned from context. Writers often considerably use sentence context clues to help the reader understand the meanings of unfamiliar words in the text (Calfee & Patrick, 1995). *Charlotte's Web* is a touching children's story of love and loss about a pig and a spider living on a farm

DOI: 10.4324/9781003130758-12

(White, 1963). In the book, the author uses context clues to help the reader. For example, "'I was just thinking,' said Charlotte, 'that people are very gullible.' 'What does gullible mean?' 'Easy to fool,' said the spider." (p.67) and "'Well,' said her mother, 'one of the pigs is a **runt**. It's very small and weak and will never amount to anything.'" (p. 1) In *Possum Magic* (Fox, 1983), the writer also gives help to the reader; the sentence context tells the reader that ANZAC biscuit is a special kind of biscuit. To find out more about ANZAC biscuits, the pupil could read up about them – do some research, or perhaps eat one.

However, while sentence context is important it is not always helpful. Some research suggests that readers often do not infer correctly the meaning of a word from context clues (Pressley, 2000).

9.3   Concept maps help to learn new words

The web

The "web" concept map is usually to describe one thing. It has categories to partition out the meaning: superordinate (overall category), coordinate (synonyms), subordinate (examples), attributes (features), and functions (uses) – and other relevant categories (e.g., history). The teacher could use a web concept map to explain the concept of "ANZAC biscuits" – see Figure 9.1.

- overall category – a baked biscuit
- synonym – a kind of cookie
- history – people baked these biscuits to raise funds for the Australia-New Zealand World War 1 effort 1914–1918
- features – made from rolled oats, sugar, butter, and golden syrup

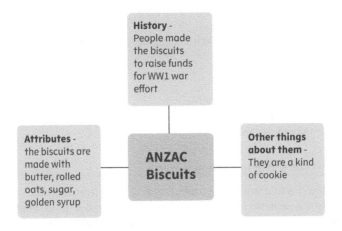

Figure 9.1 Web Concept Map for ANZAC Biscuits

The teacher could use a web concept map for an unfamiliar word like "sarcophagus":

- overall category – it is a burial place
- synonyms – it is a kind of coffin
- examples – sarcophagi were used in ancient Egypt, Rome, Greece
- features – made of stone, often with a sculpture attached or decorated in some way

The weave

The weave concept map would be useful to build knowledge about different topics in terms of similarities and differences. For example, the teacher might use a weave to compare cities mentioned in *Possum Magic* – see Table 9.1.

Table 9.1 Weave Concept Map – Comparison of Different Australian Cities.

City	Location	Size	Features
Adelaide	South Australia	1.3 million	Capital city of the state City of Music Beaches Museums
Melbourne	Southeastern Australia	5 million+	Capital city of Victoria City Trams Melbourne Cricket Ground Markets Melbourne Zoo
Brisbane	South East Queensland	2.6 million	Capital city of the state Located on Brisbane River Australia Zoo Sports

The thermometer concept map

This structure can show a range of synonyms for movements (e.g., walk, stride, run, and sprint), feelings (e.g., pleased, happy, and ecstatic), temperature (e.g., brisk, cold, and freezing), etc. The thermometer structure is like a scale or a spectrum that shows a range of meaning from low to high. For example, if the class' favourite soccer team had a surprise loss in an important game, feelings might vary from a mild "surprise" on the low end of the scale, to "sad" in the middle of the scale, to "shocked" at the high end of the scale.

Lower ---Higher
surprise   *sad*   *shocked*

Or, students may be training for the school cross country. The teacher may brainstorm how they feel when they finish their training run. The words can then be placed in order from "exhausted" at one end of the scale to "fine" at the other end of the scale. It is important that students are able to discuss the placement of the words. They may have different opinions!

Exhausted
Worn-out
Tired
Weary
Ok
Fine

Or, students could be discussing their emotions about the class trip to the local zoo, wildlife refuge or farm. The teacher could record their feelings on the whiteboard and then place them in order (e.g., excited, nervous, worried, happy, and scared).

Excited
Happy
Nervous
Worried
Scared

A thermometer diagram can be useful for students to think about exactly what word would be the best fit for the text or for their writing. It teaches children that there is a choice of words open to the writer that are slightly different but have a similar core meaning.

9.4   Dictionary/thesaurus

Dictionary

A dictionary contains all the words of a language in alphabetical order and explains the meanings of these words. The dictionary will explain that an **ANZAC biscuit** is a small baked unleavened cake; a **penguin** is a bird, does not fly, and uses wings as flippers; a **tripod** is "stilts on a camera" (one child's definition) or a "three-legged stand for supporting a camera" (more formal explanation).

Thesaurus

A thesaurus, like the dictionary, contains the words of the language, and in alphabetical order, but it gives one or more synonyms for each word. The dictionary and thesaurus are huge repositories of word knowledge. A thesaurus has synonyms for many words, e.g., **biscuit** = cake, cookie, cracker, wafer; **sweltering** = hot, tropical, baking, boiling, roasting, sizzling, scorching, torrid, stifling, suffocating, airless, oppressive, sultry, clammy, muggy, steamy, sticky, humid.

Multiple meanings

The dictionary helps with homophones and homonyms that have multiple meanings. The dictionary is not sufficient on its own because context plays an important role when determining the meaning intended for a word but the dictionary gives a strong direction for understanding the meaning. For example, the word *date* has multiple meanings, e.g., it may refer to a specified day of the month or to food used in cooking.

Johnson et al. (1983) found that 70% of the 9000 most common words in English had multiple meanings. Let's consider the word *toast*. A common definition of the word *toast* would be bread heated in a toaster. Consider what a student would be thinking if this was their only understanding of the word and their teacher said, "I went to a wedding over the weekend and we toasted the bride." It is important, when teaching vocabulary, to be explicit about common everyday words that have multiple meanings.

9.5 Word analysis – morphemes

> Anglo-Saxon – compound words, e.g., **river/bank, book/shelf.**
> Latin words – prefix/root word/suffix structure, e.g., **inter-rupt-ion**

Word analysis is the teacher demonstrating how to break words down into component morphemes – i.e., the smallest units of meaning. Being able to break words into morphemes helps to understand the word. When teaching word analysis, it is helpful to know that English consists of three historical layers.

The Anglo-Saxon layer of English vocabulary consists of everyday words such as *dog, bed, house, room, table*. Words in this layer are usually of one and two syllables. Although the words are simple, the Anglo-Saxons enriched their language by compounding two real words (e.g., *bed + room = bedroom*), or by adding to the base word with prefixes (e.g., *under-, un-*) and suffixes (*-s, -ed, -ing, -ly, -er, -est*). Anglo-Saxon words are the words that early years students encounter in their readers.

Possum Magic (Fox, 1983) has several compound words from the Anglo-Saxon layer (e.g., breakfast, something). Rosie's Walk (Hutchins, 1998) also has compound words for children to consider (e.g., beehive and haycock). In many compound words, both parts are related to its meaning, but in some compound words only one part is related to the meaning of the word, e.g., *strawberry* (type of berry), *ladybug* (type of bug) – or no part, e.g., *skyscraper* (very tall building).

The Latin vocabulary layer consists of sophisticated words. These are words associated with learning (e.g., *corruption, structure, hospitable*). An eight-year-old skilled reader may encounter an increasing number of Latin-based words in their reading (e.g., the Harry Potter books have many Latin-based words, such as the character *Voldemort*). Latin-based words like *disruption* often consist of a root word (e.g., *-rupt*), a prefix (e.g., *dis-*), and a suffix (e.g., *-ion*). The root word carries the major meaning of the word (*-rupt* means broken or burst). The word *invisible* in the *Possum Magic* story derives from Latin and uses affixation (prefix, root word, suffix). By separating the affixes (prefixes and suffixes) from the root (or stem) word, the teacher can explain their meanings: *in* - means 'not', *vis* - means 'to see', and '- *ible* indicates an adjective. Thus, the word *invisible* is an adjective meaning "not able to be seen."

An eight-year-old skilled reader may also come across words from the Greek layer, the smallest layer of English vocabulary. Words in the Greek layer tend to be specialised words, academic words, mostly in science (e.g., *geology, psychology, agoraphobia*). Words in the Greek layer consist of two Greek combining forms (or stem words), both carry the major meaning of the word (e.g., *geo-* and *-logy*).

9.6   Reading books improves vocabulary

In many classrooms, on most days, teachers read children's picture books, novels, and/or poems to the class. When they do, it is an excellent opportunity to expose students to new vocabulary as well as an excellent chance to teach vocabulary. An example of this with five-year-olds would be the book *Rosie's Walk* (Hutchins, 1998). In the story, Rosie the hen goes for a walk and a fox follows her. As she walks, she passes a pond, a mill, and a haycock/haystack.

Juel et al. (2003) described how at the end of the reading of *Rosie's Walk*, there is an opportunity for the teacher to go back to the book and discuss the meanings of some of the more unfamiliar words. The teacher may have already written the words *pond, mill*, and *haycock* on cards. The words are a little different and many children may not know them. Juel et al. suggested that by learning new words in context this way, the teacher is "anchoring" the words (p. 13).

The word cards showed the spelling of the words; the story gave a context for the words; and the teacher helped students to clarify any questions they had about the words. In Juel et al., they found that it helped the less skilled readers if the teacher reviewed the phoneme and phonics patterns in the words, e.g., the *ay* in *haycock*. The idea of anchoring is that the student can store words in memory in multiple ways that bond to each other, both meaning and spelling, and this acts as a kind of glue to remember the words.

Reading to children is particularly important in the early years of schooling. The reason is that young children are learning to decode and the words they encounter in the early readers are usually already part of their vocabulary. These words are usually familiar words. To learn new words and enhance children's vocabulary in the early school curriculum, we can introduce them to new vocabulary by reading to them and discussing the unfamiliar vocabulary in picture books, novels, and poetry. Hirsch (2016) argued that in "the earliest grades, learning by being read aloud to and through talking and listening is fundamental to language progress and needs to receive great emphasis" (p. 168). It is critically important for teachers to consider how best to speed up the growth of vocabulary. Reading interesting books to children and discussing vocabulary is one way.

Nagy (2005) argued that "effective vocabulary instruction needs to be long-term and comprehensive" (p. 27). What is meant by this is that vocabulary instruction needs to occur daily throughout the year. There is no quick fix/or quick way to increase vocabulary. The teacher cannot simply say, "Today we are going to learn 50 words." It is not realistic; it is not going to happen. Vocabulary acquisition is a slow process. The rewards, however, are great. Vocabulary is critical for academic success.

The research on teaching vocabulary indicates that teachers can only properly teach 300–400 unfamiliar words in a school year (Cervetti et al., 2023). There are two problems teachers face in teaching vocabulary. First is the problem of transfer. Learning several new words from one specific text or story can definitely help children to learn those specific words. The problem is that the learning may not help when they come to another book that has more new words. Second is the problem that the words we teach in class may not be the words they will meet on standardised tests (Elleman et al., 2009). Why is this? The conundrum is that every new text has different words. It is impossible to predict what words will be in standardised tests or national assessments like NAPLAN. There are so many words out there. The words in one text are unlikely to be in the next. This is the challenge for the teacher.

On the positive side, teaching vocabulary is an important thing to do, it will build more knowledge of words and there are other equally important reasons to teach children about words. One of them is to instil a love of words. Teachers can do this through their own inspiring and passionate teaching of word meanings and of ways to learn words. Every school day presents opportunities to do this.

There are other reasons to be optimistic. Picture books and other school reading material are rich in vocabulary and children will learn new words from context clues as they read for themselves or listen to audio books. In the early years of school the teacher will need to step up and be a surrogate reader for children in their class until these beginner readers can decode text on their own. They will rely on the teacher to help them build their vocabulary by reading books to them, and explaining words to them. The school day provides many opportunities to read to and talk with children.

Let's return to *Rosie's Walk*. In many classrooms, it is likely that students will not be familiar with words like "haycock," "pond," or "mill," but if the teacher reads picture books to them regularly, and discusses words with them, the impact of these multiple exposures to new words, across the school year, will ensure that words like "haycock," "pond," or "mill" become well known.

Consider these phrases from the classic picture book, *Edward the Emu* (Knowles, 1988) "being an emu was frankly a bore" and "life was certainly grand for a lion in his den." It is unlikely young children will have an understanding of the words *frankly*, *bore*, *grand*, and *den* but they will be exposed to these words when the teacher reads to them and through context clues and discussion they will learn them. We discussed in Chapter 7 that it is only after multiple exposures to a word that the word becomes well known.

9.7   Conclusion

Teaching vocabulary knowledge directly is a challenge for the teacher. Which words to choose? How best to teach the words? This chapter has suggested that the most important thing for pupils to learn is to learn the technical language associated with working out the meanings of new words. We suggested that this technical language applies to four main ways to learn words – context clues, concept maps, the dictionary and thesaurus, and word analysis.

Teaching vocabulary is worthwhile even though the teaching may not transfer easily to standardised tests. Such tests sample from a huge range of words. The main thing is that unfamiliar vocabulary crops up in nearly every text children read so it is worth teaching vocabulary. Growing children's vocabulary in a significant way will not happen overnight but it will happen if we make it happen by taking every opportunity to teach about words.

Encouraging pupils to read as much as possible, to focus on content words that they do not know the meanings of, to use the learning suggestions outlined in this chapter, such as context clues, concept maps, word analysis, and the dictionary – this will give them self-agency and success.

Part IV
Writing

10 Writing

What is it?

10.1 Introduction

A five-year-old writes a one-sentence story, "We went to the zoo" and shows it to the teacher. They have written a nice beginning but it is not finished. They need to write more. The teacher says to the child, "It is a nice story, a nice beginning but how are you going to finish it, can you add some more events, and an ending?" The child goes away and, 15 minutes later, has written "We went to the zoo. We saw the monkeys and lions. We went on the swings. We had a fun day." It showed we can teach even very young children how to put structure into their work, simply by asking a few questions that will keep the writing going, about the importance of an attention-grabbing beginning, a middle that has substance, and a strong end that speaks to the reader.

Most young children know how to write but they do not know how to compose. They have powerful ideas but what they write is often incomplete or incoherent. Their work lacks structure. We need to teach them how to organise their thoughts and present them in a coherent way.

What is the formula for becoming an effective writer? Skilled writing consists of interesting ideas well presented. Skilled writing has coherence, an effective argument, and is well-structured. In addition, skilled writing requires excellent handwriting and spelling skills – neat and accurate presentation. Delivering on all these goals is a real challenge for the teacher – but you can do it!

This chapter covers

- The simple view of writing
- Can teachers teach writing?
- Teaching narrative writing
- Teaching expository writing

10.2 The simple view of writing

Writing is a multi-component process involving spelling, vocabulary, grammar, general knowledge, a sense of audience, knowledge of how to structure

DOI: 10.4324/9781003130758-14

ideas, and ideas themselves. The writer needs creativity to compose a text, a willingness to come up with interesting ideas, and to organise the ideas in a convincing way.

All writers are not the same. Among young writers there are many differences. Skilled writers, compared with developing writers produce a higher quality of writing, better organised writing, make more use of structure in their writing, use richer vocabulary, and write more (Graham et al., 2017).

In story writing, a developing writer might have a similar set of ideas to a skilled writer but the skilled writer is able to enrich their writing, giving it more quality by describing the characters in more detail, giving more information about the setting, and having a strong beginning and ending. Skilled writers write more. When they write more, they receive higher grades (Graham et al., 2017). Longer pieces of work get better marks. Some say that less is more, but in children's writing, this is not always the case.

The simple view of writing (Berninger et al., 2002; Juel et al., 1986; Yeung et al., 2017) theorises that any differences between skilled and less skilled writers boil down to two things. The first is ideas. The writer needs interesting ideas. A piece of writing will never stand up unless it has something interesting to say. The second is accurate spelling. Spelling includes not only writing words correctly but also having neat and legible handwriting. Handwriting is important in the early years of school. If you cannot read a younger student's handwriting, then you cannot read their ideas (Connelly et al., 2019; James & Berninger, 2019).

Research on the simple view of writing has found that ideas and spelling (including handwriting) account for most of the variance in writing skills in the first year of school, with spelling very important. After that, once children become more fluent in spelling and handwriting, ideas become what determines the quality of writing (Berninger et al., 2002; Juel et al., 1986; Juel, 1988; Shanahan, 1984).

The model says that writing difficulties are not all the same. There are different kinds of writing difficulties. Some children write well because they spell well and have compelling ideas (the writer). Others have compelling ideas but cannot spell (such as students with dyslexia). Others can spell but have difficulty articulating their ideas (perhaps an English Language Learner). Some have difficulty with spelling and ideas. The categories (ideas, spelling) are not black and white; they are on a spectrum, and children may be on the lower or higher end of each category.

This means that if there are issues in children's writing, it must be caused either by spelling, ideas, or both – see Figure 10.1.

When the teacher peruses children's writing efforts, they need to think of the simple view, of ideas and spelling, to figure out what the main issue is. Is it because spelling and handwriting are illegible? Is it because their ideas are jumbled or non-existent? Is it because of both these factors?

Figure 10.1 The Simple View of Writing

10.3 Can teachers teach writing?

Many teachers feel unprepared to teach writing. Over half of teachers think that their initial teacher training did not prepare them well enough to teach writing (Brenner & McQuirk, 2019; Wyatt-Smith et al., 2018). It may explain why some teacher comments on children's writing mention spelling and punctuation but not how to improve the content of writing. It may explain why many schools do not devote much time to writing. In the US, it is fewer than 10 minutes a day (Cutler & Graham, 2008). In Australia, the situation is similar (Malpique et al., 2023).

On the other hand, reviews of the research on teaching writing, using meta-analysis statistics, have found that teaching writing helps children to progress (e.g., Graham et al., 2012). Teaching how to compose effective writing, e.g., using an effective text structure, using a planner – these help to improve the quality of writing (McMaster et al., 2018). Teaching writing is better than not teaching it. This "teaching something" factor is important. It is worth spending time teaching writing on a regular basis. Children are likely to benefit.

10.4 Narrative writing

Baynton (1995) was of the opinion that in the first years of school, children's story writing lacked structure. Baynton wrote that children's stories often consist of "and then, and then, and then." To stop this from happening, teachers need to ask young writers to think about stories in terms of a problem. Ask what the problem will be about and who has the problem. Then the story structure "falls into place" (p. 6). The next section describes the components of a narrative structure for writing effective stories – see also the two different story planners, one simple and the other more sophisticated, in Chapter 12, Figures 12.1 and 12.2.

The 4 basic elements of a narrative

Every narrative (or story) needs a problem but in addition there are other components that make an effective story. There are FOUR parts to a story: character, plot, setting, and theme. These are the building blocks (Calfee & Patrick, 1995; Dymock, 2007; Nicholson & Dymock, 2018). They apply to fairy tales and to Shakespeare. The life of the story is in the plot and the characters:

1. Setting – tells when and where and the mood, the atmosphere. The writer has to draw a picture in words of when and where the story will take place, and the atmosphere (or mood).
2. Characters – are what draw the reader to the story. They are the foundation of the story. Readers engage with interesting characters who have unusual personalities and ways of thinking about the world. Readers like characters who react differently or in a surprising way to solve problems. Every story has major characters and minor characters. The writer has to make sure the characters differ from each other in looks, personality, etc., and come alive.
3. Plot – the action of a story, is made up of a series of events. In each event, the characters have a problem and they move from one event to another to find a solution. Students could use a planner to sketch out the plot. It could be a story graph planner or an episode analysis planner. A story graph works for short stories, graphing the plot from low to high levels of action. The y-axis is level of action (low to high) and the x-axis is time (beginning to end). The student writes key events in the story onto the chart and then draws a line through the events to show the pathway of the plot.

   Alternatively, before writing, students can sketch out the events in the plot as a series of episodes. A series of episodes is for long stories. Each episode has a problem, reaction, action, and outcome. In short stories the plot is just one episode. With some help from the teacher, children can work out the elements in the plot. Children have an intuitive sense of boundaries between episodes, when one episode ends and another begins. This will help them to diagram the action in the plot.
4. Theme – is the message that underlies the story. The theme often explains the motives of the characters, comments on social relationships, perhaps relates to society in general. The theme may be implicit and unstated but the reader can work it out based on the main events in the story. Ask students, "Why did the author write the story?" this will encourage them to think about the theme.

Reworking a well-known or classic story

Some writers are able to re-create a well-known or classic story, give it their own voice and make it different in some interesting way, e.g., different versions of the classic story of the *Three Little Pigs* (Scieszka, 1996; Sierra, 2010). In one version, the *Three Little Wolves and the Big Bad Pig* (Trivizas, 2003) the writer reworked the story into something very different. In Episode 1, the three little wolves built a solid brick house. The big bad pig came along, tried to blow it down, and failed, so took a sledgehammer to it and knocked it down. In Episode 2, the wolves built a house made of steel with barbed wire around it, armour plates, CCTV. The pig tried to blow it down, and failed, so the pig used dynamite to blow up the house. In Episode 3, the wolves built a house made of cherry blossoms, roses, and marigolds. The pig tried to blow down the flower house but smelled the flowers, realised the harm done, and changed to become a nicer person. It was the same concept as the original fairy tale story but different and still interesting. Another twist to the classic story is *Too many pigs and one big bad wolf* (Cali & Balducci, 2022). The wolf told his version of the "big bad wolf" story. The wolf's story was just one sentence, "Once upon a time there were three little pigs and the wolf ate them." Baynton (1995) would probably say, "Where is the problem?" and this was the message of the picture book, that the wolf was not giving enough information about the problem, about what actually happened. In the picture book, the wolf had to keep expanding the story until it was more like the conventional story.

Children are very imaginative and may be able to make up their own version of the *Three Little Pigs* story with a different twist to the plot. This is what happened in the story below, written by an eight-year-old. The child started by writing a brief planner for the story, sketching out the characteristics of the major characters (pig, wolves) and the problem that the story had to solve. The child then wrote the story. The planner and story (with the original spelling) are below:

Planner:
Three little wolfs and the big bad pig
pig – bad
wolfs – good
Problem – pig keeps stealing baby wolfs and eating them

Story:

Once upon a time there lived a pig and he liked wolfs not as friends but as stew. When he was little he sang this song wolf stew wolf stew yummy yummy wolf stew. One day the pig that we will call piggy came to a stray house. He said little wolf little wolf let me come in. Not by the tail of my rump replyed the first little wolf. Soon piggy came to a house made of wood. He noked on the door and said little wolf little wolf let me come in. Not by the tail of my pretty behind, she said. Piggy shot at the wolf but she escaped to her sister. Piggy followed her and do you know what the wolfs called the police and caught the pig in the act. All pigs were moved from the country and piggy was never seen agen. And every wolf was forgiven.

10.5   Expository writing

To a younger student, stories come naturally but descriptive writing does not. Non-fiction writing is very different to writing stories. In non-fiction, the writer must explain, inform, interpret, define, and persuade. As we noted in the chapters on reading comprehension, there are two main kinds of expository writing, descriptive and sequential, and each kind of writing can have several different structures depending on the topic (Dymock, 2005; Nicholson & Dymock, 2018). The next section gives short descriptions of these kinds of texts – for planners to use, see Chapter 12, Figures 12.4 to 12.9.

Descriptive writing

The **list** structure is for the kind of writing where it is not possible to organise the information into subtopics. The information is in no particular order, such as writing a list of ten things a tourist can see in London. The tourist list might describe Trafalgar Square, Buckingham Palace, Sherlock Holmes' house in 221 Baker Street, Charles Dickens Museum, and so on. Another kind of list might be of unusual but interesting sports like walking backwards or egg and spoon racing. It might be a list of items found in a sparrow's nest. In list structure writing, the list does not have to be in any specific order.

The **web** structure is for writing about one topic. It might be about a specific bird, e.g., the kookaburra. It might be about a product, a country, a person. Any one, single topic could take a web structure form. In the case of the kookaburra, the web might have subtopics like its features, habitat, diet, and enemies. One way to think about the web structure is that it looks like a spider web with its different categories.

A **weave** structure is for writing about similarities and differences of two or more subjects. It might be a comparison of the bush sparrow and the house sparrow. The bush sparrow eats seeds and the house sparrow eats aphids. The two birds differ in colour, and other things. The writing could compare the birds in terms of their appearance, diet, and "other things." One way to think of a weave structure is that it is like a matrix.

A **hierarchy** structure is for classification-type writing. You start with a general category and move down to subcategories. For example, the top of the hierarchy could be animals, the next level down birds, insects, etc. The next level down for birds would be kinds of birds – sparrows, seagulls, pigeons, hawks, etc. One way to think of a hierarchy is like an upside down tree.

Sequential writing

A **sequence** structure is for writing about a step-by-step process, like making a cup of tea or milking a cow. If a pupil brought to school a plastic tub of silkworms munching on leaves, the class report would follow a life-cycle sequence structure, from caterpillar to moth. One way to think about a sequence structure is like a flow chart. In a sequence structure the writing describes a process, one thing leads to another.

A different kind of sequence structure is for writing about a **problem-solution** situation, such as saving a historic house by moving it from a flood-prone area to higher ground. Another kind of sequence writing might be to describe a **cause-effect** situation, e.g., where lightning hits a gum tree and the tree dies, leaving some animals without their food source.

Persuasive writing

Persuasive writing has its own structure. In this kind of writing the goal is to persuade an audience to buy something, change something, or agree with you, e.g., should we make school uniforms compulsory; should we eliminate homework. Writers who can persuade are able to consider the audience and predict how well the audience will receive their ideas. These are the skills of persuasion. The skills involve being aware that the audience might disagree and being aware that opinions will differ.

In persuasion writing, the writer needs to think about the topic, pick one side or the other, and write reasons to support their point of view. A simple structure might be

- Start with an interesting opening line that reels in the audience straight away
- Then cut to the action with at least three reasons to support your argument
- End with a satisfying conclusion – try to get the audience on your side with a personal plea or a prediction, or simply sum up what you have said

10.6 Conclusion

Students often have amazing ideas for writing but do not know how to structure their ideas on paper. Effective writing needs structure. This chapter has focused on structure as the best way to improve children's writing. Even younger students can benefit from planning their writing. We can teach them how narrative and expository writing works. We can start in a simple way, with a simple planner and build up from there. The research says that teaching students to structure their writing will improve the quality. Planning writing encourages the writer to look at the big picture, to pause before jumping in, to know what they want to say, and to write in an organised and convincing way that engages the reader.

11 Assessing writing

11.1 Introduction

Kyla's school report said that her writing made, "good use of vivid adjectives, powerful verbs, varied sentence beginnings, engaging hooks, effective dialogue, and creative ideas." Yet the report gave Kyla a below-average grade for her writing. Her parents were bemused. What was missing from her writing that meant she got a lower grade? What did she need to do to improve? From the teacher's point of view, however, it may be that Kyla's writing despite all its positive features, somehow did not create an impact. What is it that gives impact to writing? How can we assess the components of effective writing?

This chapter covers

- Standardised assessment of writing
- Informal assessment of writing
- Adding structure to writing
- Writing for impact
- Assessing and giving feedback

11.2 Standardised assessment of writing

Standardised assessment measures are the most accurate ways to assess the quality of writing of children. A measure that fits younger students is the *Test of Early Written Language-3* (TEWL) (Hresko et al., 2012). It is for students aged 4–11 years. In this test, children write a story. The story prompt is a picture of an event that the student then has to write about.

When assessing children's writing skills in TEWL, the marker scores both presentation and ideas. For presentation, there are points for spelling, number of sentences written, paragraphing, and so on. For ideas, there are points for an attention-getting beginning, inclusion of setting, characters, an engaging plot, and a satisfying ending. The student gets extra points if any of the following elements occur in the story: characters show emotion, the plot is interesting, the story ending is clever, and the words "sparkle."

A problem for the classroom teacher who would like to use TEWL to assess writing is not just the cost but that to purchase the test, the teacher needs to have a

DOI: 10.4324/9781003130758-15

special qualification in testing procedures. Accessing the test may not be possible for the teacher if they do not have this training. This is the case for many standardised tests, they require specialist training. Most classroom teachers will be unable to access such tests. A possible solution is for the school to hire a trained assessor to administer the standardised test. If this is not possible the teacher will need to use an informal measure.

11.3 Informal measures – checklists

An informal alternative to standardised measures of writing skill is for the teacher to use a checklist. The teacher can explain to students the parts of the checklist so they know what the teacher is looking for.

A checklist to assess narrative writing skills might be

- Immediately hooks the reader
- Keeps the reader wanting to read more
- Detailed setting
- Strong plot
- Characters come alive
- Interesting words, sentences, and language structure
- Engaging, personal voice

A checklist to assess expository writing skills might be

1. There is a title for the work
2. Beginning – uses a hook to catch attention of reader
3. Middle – has chunks of information – several subheadings
4. Middle – has at least 4–5 information points
5. Conclusion – speaks to the reader, reiterates the main points, has a satisfying end

11.4 Adding structure to writing

What writing qualities should children aim for at different age levels? Table 11.1 is a summary of some of the expectations mentioned in both the Australian Curriculum and the New Zealand Learning Progressions.

The expectations cover different writing structures but also other aspects of writing such as vocabulary and spelling. At ages 5–6, expectations are modest, that children use simple sentences, everyday vocabulary, phonemic spelling, correct handwriting, and basic punctuation (e.g., start with a capital letter and end with a full stop). A simple structure – a sketch of a few organising ideas – is all that is needed.

By ages 7–8, however, expectations increase markedly, children need to write in a more structured and detailed way, use complex sentences, richer and more nuanced vocabulary, accurate spelling, fast and legible handwriting, and correct punctuation. The expectations suggest that by eight years of age, children should be able to write and spell very well. Structure and planning are key.

Table 11.1 Writing Expectations – Ages 5–8.

	Ages 5–6	Ages 6–7	Ages 7–8	Age 8
Planning	Simple sketch	Plan	Detailed plan	Planner, subheads
Structure		Stories, reports, recounts		Argument, Persuasion
Organisation			On topic, relevant content	Main ideas, relevant detail
Presentation		Revise, edit, proofread	Revise, edit, proofread	Revise, edit, proofread
Grammar	Simple/compound sentences, e.g., using *and/but*	Verb-subject agreement	Consistent tense	Linking words
Vocabulary	Everyday vocabulary	Precise verbs, nouns, adjectives	More precise	More sophisticated words – prefixes and suffixes
Figurative language			Alliteration	Similes and onomatopoeia
Punctuation	Capital letters, full stops	Capital letters, full stops	Exclamation and question marks	Speech marks, commas, apostrophes
Spelling	Phonemic spelling	Phonemic spelling	Correct spelling	Correct spelling
Handwriting	Accurate	Accurate	Fast, automatic	

11.5   Writing effectively

To write effectively, students need to use structure. Successful writers plan and structure their writing to the last detail. Presentation (spelling, handwriting) is important but the ideas have to be good. There has to be something interesting to write about. Otherwise, it will fail to impress.

By eight years of age, children are expected to write in a sophisticated way, as can be seen in the writing expectations for writing tasks in national assessment tests like NAPLAN. For example, in one NAPLAN task for seven-year-olds, children had to write an imaginative story. They had to choose one of several illustrations to write about. The illustrations were of a girl with a backpack, a frog, a man with a pointy nose, a magical goat character. Students also had to choose an item from a list of illustrated objects (a canoe, a pair of boots, a magical lamp, a book) and imagine that the character they chose found that object and something magical happened. The instructions for writing the content were as follows – think about characters, think of a complication to the story, think about how the story will end. The instructions for writing style were as follows – plan, choose words carefully, write in sentences, check accuracy of spelling, punctuation, and paragraphing, and do an overall edit when finished writing.

In addition to having a structure for the writing, the expectations were to use a planner, write on topic, revise, proofread, use dialogue, use figurative speech, and produce fast and accurate handwriting.

Looking at the demands of the NAPLAN task, it shows that much progress in the craft of writing is expected from young writers in the first few years of school. For some children this is indeed the case, as in the following story written by an eight-year-old. It was a story about penguins who escaped captivity.

> Life in the fast lane
>
> Once upon a time, there lived six little penguins they were tired of the zoo. One day they had a plan. When everyone arrived in the morning they played dead. Everyone went to the funeral in the open sea. They put the bodies in the water and to their surprise the penguins jumped up and swam away. The people called animal control. So the penguins were free in the ocean. What I haven't mentioned reader is that the penguins are very intelligent they can talk and as you might already know can play dead. The penguins' names are Chicken, Fish, Sardine, Sausage, Noodles, and the team leader Boss. "Boss what are we going to do now?" said Sardine. "Now," said Boss, "now we are going to find a safe place. The animal control are after us so we must be extra sneaky." The penguins swam away and were never bothered again. The end.

It was an impressive story. The story had a title. The opening hooked in the reader with the penguins saying they were bored. The story had structure. It had a setting (zoo), characters (six penguins), and a plot (problem – bored, action – they pretend to be dead, outcome – they escape). There was an unstated theme that if trapped in a situation you do not like, it is possible to escape your situation. The theme of the story was a positive message.

The above story showed that children can make huge strides in writing in just a few years of work. The challenge for the teacher is how to enable all children to make such progress – and more.

11.6   Assessing children's writing and giving feedback

"Dear Gramma, Thank you for the cookies. They were good. What else can I say?" This line, from a Peanuts cartoon (Schultz, 2000, p. 159), where Lucy writes to thank her grandmother, shows us that sometimes it is difficult to say what you want to say (Zinsser, 2006). Yet sometimes a small but positive comment from the teacher is important feedback to the young writer, to give them direction, boost their self-confidence, and take them forward (Buckingham & Goodall, 2019). In the following examples of children's writing, the teacher tries to give short feedback but with a positive direction to help increase the effectiveness of the writing.

Writing sample of a five-year-old

mi gran has bAn her Sm Tims she Ring me and she says vr is a shep on the lon but she is tesing.

The teacher could say, "I really liked how you said your Gran has brown hair and sometimes phones you and teases you about sheep being on the lawn. Can you write some more about your Gran?" The pupil might be able to go back and write some more.

Writing sample of a six-year-old

Tonight my mothr is haveing a tupawer party. A tupawer party is not for children. A tupawer party goes like this. The adolts sit down and tok about plastic stuff in the kichin. It is not like a kids party.

The teacher could say, "What wonderful writing about how an adult Tupperware party is not like a children's party. So interesting. Can you write a little more about the party?"

Writing sample of a seven-year-old

The writing task was to report on the over-fishing of whitebait and glass eels in New Zealand, where dams stop glass eels (juveniles) from migrating and koi carp eat the whitebait. Whitebait are not in Australia, but there is a similar fish called "sandy sprat," 5 cm long.

White bait and glass eels

There are two difrint kinds of white bait. There is white bait fish and white bait eels. Lots of people like to eat white bait and glass eels. The white bait fishing season is between 15 August and 30 November. This report will talk about the problems with over fishing and some saloshons. Some of the problems the glass eels have is when they go down streem to get to the river, because the dams stop them from getting to the river. One of the white baits Problems is the white bait get cort by the koi and cap when they try to get to the sea. One of the solutions is something calld an eel Ladder. It is like steping stones but with rests and hideing spots. One solution for the cap and koi is a speshill trap. Onle cap and koi can go in to the trap then they suffocate them and they are tornd into dog food. As you know white bait and glass eels have had some problems. We need to protekt our treasures or they will go extinkt.

The teacher might say, "I am so impressed with the way you did research for this report and your real concern for helping these fish to survive. It was a very good opening, you hooked in the reader. I liked the way you used a problem-solution structure to write about the problems for these fish and then how you described the solutions."

Writing sample of an eight-year-old – the writing prompt was the word "banana."

Far away on a stradid iland there were 2 foxes sitting down on the beach. The iland was small and quite hot as well. No one knew how these two little foxes fond them selfs there. Now on this iland there was a banana tree with one singula dilishos jusey banana and this was a problem because there were two foxes and one banana.

The teacher might say, "I really liked the very imaginative and humorous story line with the desert island and two foxes. Do you think you could add a little more to tell us how they solved their problem?"

11.7   Conclusion

Assessing writing in the early years is essential to monitor academic and personal progress. There are standardised assessment measures to use, but there are also informal ways to assess writing progress and give feedback. Teacher observation and feedback during writing lessons is one form of informal assessment. Another informal measure is to use a checklist. Students can use checklists as well, to check that they have included all the important elements in their writing.

Assessment is not just about gathering data but feeding it back to students to help them with their writing. Students will benefit from teacher feedback. Feedback does not have to be detailed. Even a simple suggestion from the teacher, like "Can you add a little more detail to your story/report?" can help a lot. It will add structure and coherence and these can make children's writing more effective.

12   Teaching writing

12.1   Introduction

Young children often have interesting ideas but find it hard to structure their ideas into a coherent piece of writing. Their work reads like stream of consciousness, which is authentic and natural but somehow lacks substance, feels incomplete. We will look at some simple ideas for teaching how to write in a more compelling way. Planning out the structure of what you want to write before starting is the key to effective writing.

Writers need to draw on the right structure for the task. Most children have an intuitive idea about the structure of a story, e.g., "once upon a time ... and they lived happily ever after" but expository writing, such as reports, speeches, recounts, and so on are not like stories. They use different structures. In this chapter, we explain how all these structures work.

This chapter covers

- Using WH questions for writing
- Writing sentences
- Teaching narrative writing
- Teaching expository structure
- Teaching persuasive writing
- Effective presentation of writing
- Beyond the first sentence – how to get started in writing

12.2   WH questions can help the beginner writer

Asking WH questions can help beginners build structure into their writing. An example of this was a Year 1 classroom in a disadvantaged school. Most of the class were from minority and immigrant backgrounds. Many of the children were not yet writing on their own. They needed help. The teacher encouraged each child to tell the class what they did on the weekend. As they did this, the teacher asked others in the class to help them expand their ideas. For example, one child

DOI: 10.4324/9781003130758-16

said that she went to the supermarket. Then other children asked WH questions, e.g., when did you go, why did you go, who did you go with, what did you buy? Pupils initially produced a one-idea, one-sentence "recount" of an event on the weekend, but the WH questions helped them to add more sentences. Some examples of the impact of WH questions on their "recounts" of what they did on the weekend are as follows:

- I went to the supermarket. To get bread and eggs. With my sister.
- I went to the shop. To get some smokes. For my mum.
- I went to the football. On Saturday. In the car. With mum and dad.
- I went to church. With my mum. On Sunday.
- I went to rugby training. With my mum and dad.
- I went to my dancing practice.
- I went to the hospital. To see nana.
- I went to the shop. With mum and dad. To get a bike. For my sister. It was purple.

The writing they finally produced was a result of asking WH questions. They were simple recounts, but there was some structure. The basic elements were there, showing a sequence of events. The WH questions had enabled each student to create more interesting work.

12.3 Writing sentences

A beginner writer may slump on the desk with the frustration of not being able to write more than one sentence. Sometimes, though, the teacher asking one or two simple questions may help the student to keep going, e.g., "Can you also write what colour is your bike, and where do you keep it at home?" (Schulz, 2009).

Sometimes it helps to explain to the class in a more formal way the parts of a sentence. We speak sentences, but often we do not know how we do that. One idea is to explain that a sentence tells us *Who did What to Whom*. The student then starts with "who" (the noun subject), adds the "did what" (the verb), and then the "to whom" (the object).

An alternate definition of a sentence would be a person or thing (noun – start of sentence) does something (verb) at a certain time and place and for a reason (when, where, why – end of sentence). Some examples might be

Person or thing	Does something	When, where, why
Anna	plays tennis	after school.
Our cat	watches television	if it is an animal show.
A package	came yesterday	to our house.
The rocket	exploded	in the air.

12.4   Teaching narrative writing

Every writer of a story has a problem. Every story is about solving a problem. It has to be an interesting problem to be an interesting story. In terms of nuts and bolts, a story has to say who did what to whom, when, where, why, and what it all means (i.e., the message, the point of the story).

Story writing is not about real life, but the story may have its origins in real events or imagined events. Stories nearly all have a generic structure – see Table 12.1. There are four components to a story – setting, characters, plot, and theme (Dymock, 2007) – see also Figures 12.2 and 12.3.

- Setting is the "where and when." The story has to give the reader a sense of time and place – and atmosphere or mood.
- Characters are the "who," either major or minor or both. Characters should not be just of list of names without any life in them. The story has to make the characters come alive. It has to show their features and personality, and some reason for us to like them or not.
- Plot is the "what" of the story, and it has one or more episodes. A plot consists of episodes. An episode has four parts: the problem, how the characters respond to the problem, the action they take to solve the problem, and the outcome.
- Complications add to the plot. A complication is some obstacle to solving the problem that the characters have to get around.
- Theme is the message, the moral of the story, and the point of the story.

Table 12.1 Story Web Structure – Four Components of a Story.

Setting	Characters	Plot	Theme
Time	Major	• Problem	Message
Place	Minor	• Response	
Mood		• Action	
		• Complication	
		• Outcome	

By ages 6–7 years, children should be able to use a basic story planner to sketch some ideas, to make a plan – see Figure 12.1. By ages 7–8, students might use a more advanced planner – see Figure 12.2. The planner is not supposed to take up much time. It is just to sketch out some ideas, e.g., in Figure 12.3, the writing prompt was four words – *roof*, *moon*, *look*, and *train*. The student quickly sketched the elements of the story.

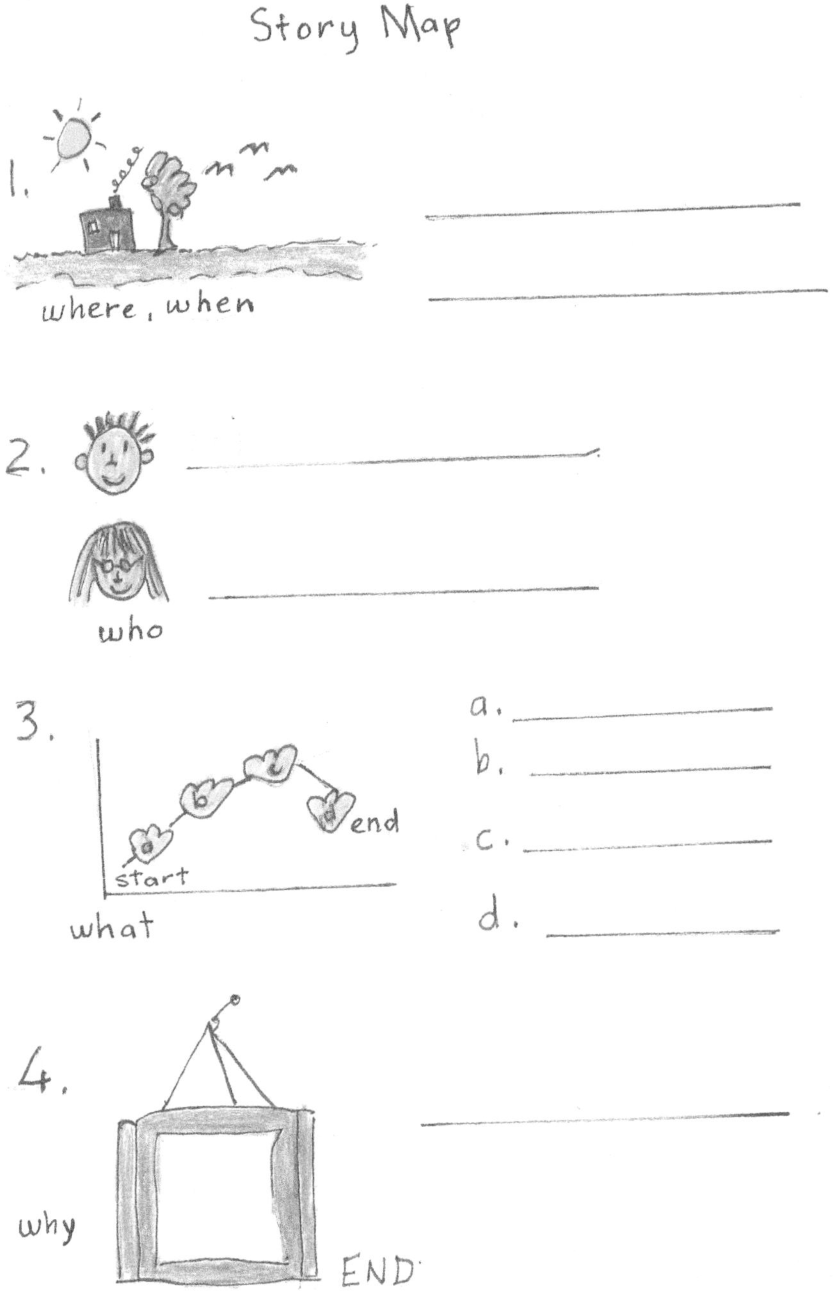
Story Map
1.
where, when
2.
who
3.
a.
b.
c.
d.
start
end
what
4.
why
END

Figure 12.1 Basic Story Planner

Figure 12.2 Proficient Story Planner

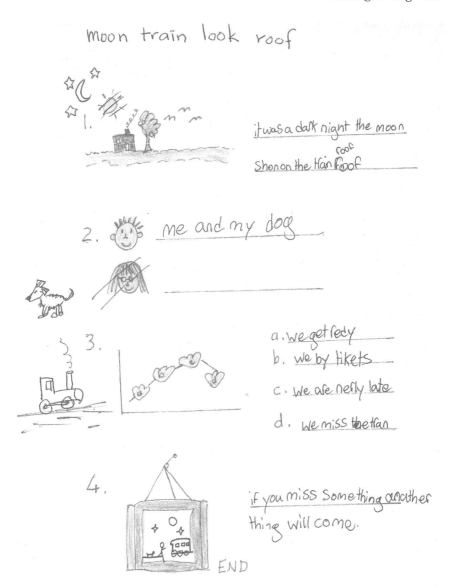

Figure 12.3 Example of Student Planner Notes for a Story

12.5 Teaching expository writing

Most expository writing has a descriptive structure, e.g., list, web, weave, and sequence. Observations of the kinds of texts read and writing done by younger children at school suggest that they do a lot of writing of descriptive and sequential (to do with time). By age 8, they are also doing persuasive writing, e.g., speeches.

Children can improve their writing by using a planner that follows the structural features of the different kinds of expository writing. The teacher can explain how planners can help students "see" the structure of what they want to write and how to write it.

Expository writing, reports, etc. can have a range of structures depending on the task (Dymock, 2005). As shown in Table 12.2, the two main expository text structures are first, descriptive, explaining one or more things in detail, and second, sequential – showing a series of steps over time.

If the student is writing about different facts or topics in no particular order, it is a list structure. If it is about one thing, it is a web structure and it needs three to four subtopics and details to go into each subtopic. If the student is writing about two or more things and comparing them, then it is a weave structure. It is a compare-contrast matrix that shows the similarities and differences between two or more ideas, things, animals, people, cities, etc. A sequence structure is different again. It shows a series of steps in a process, it could be a problem-solution sequence, or it could be a cause-effect sequence.

Explicit teaching of structures can encourage students to use these structures to improve their writing. Understanding how to structure a text helps the student to write with more coherence and in an organised way.

Table 12.2 Types of Expository Writing.

Descriptive	Sequential
List	Linear string
Web	Cause-effect
Weave	Problem-solution

Descriptive text

List

This kind of writing has no structure. Information is presented one item after the other. The items in the list do not relate to each other. This kind of writing is a list, e.g., "jobs to do," a shopping list, a list of names, a list of products made in a certain city or country, etc. Writing that involves lists are "listicles." Many magazine articles are like this – the writer lists ten places to see, five things to do when you are bored, 20 ways to lose weight, six ways to make friends, and so on. There is no clear connecting link between the items of information except that they relate to a topic. When writing a list text, encourage students to use the list structure planner – see Figure 12.4.

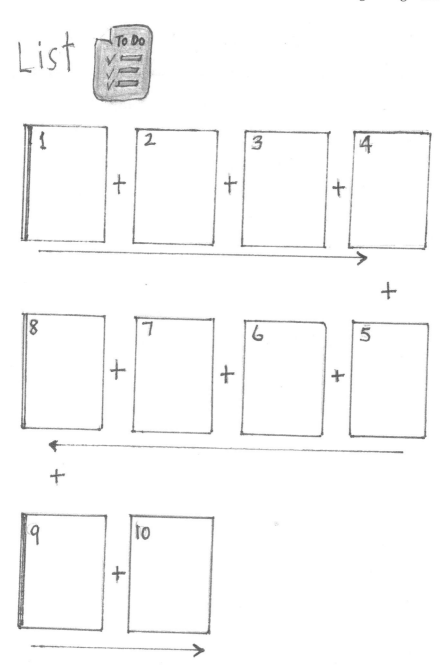

Figure 12.4 List Planner

Web

This kind of writing is about ONE topic and describes it in some detail. When the class brainstorms ideas about a topic, such as "dogs" it starts with what seems like a random list of things but then it seems the list breaks into categories. For example, a brainstorm about Tasmanian tigers might break into subcategories like habitat, diet, features, and enemies. Another example might be to write about the Eastern Rosella. It has very colourful feathers. Its habitat is in holes in forest trees. Its food includes insects but mainly it eats plants, e.g., they even eat thistles. Its call is "twink twink." The web can add other details like weight (120 g), length (33 cm), and lifespan (ten years). The important decision when deciding to use a web structure is to make sure you are writing about ONE thing – see the web planner in Figure 12.5.

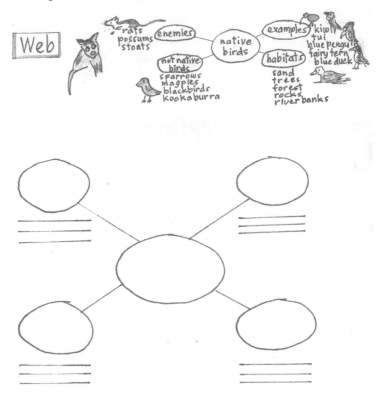

Figure 12.5 Web Planner

Weave

This kind of writing is about TWO or more topics. The structure of the text is compare-contrast. It might be a comparison of cities like Sydney and Melbourne in terms of population, location, products made, public transport, sports facilities, tourist attractions, history, weather, and so on. Or, a weave structure might compare and contrast three different brands of roller skates – in terms of price, safety rating, comfort, and reliability. Or, a weave structure might compare and contrast different birds (e.g., sparrows, owls, seagulls) in terms of features, habitat, diet, and so on. The web can give insights, e.g., birds' habitats reflect diet. Birds often nest where they can best access food, e.g., seagulls near the sea and eagles on high cliffs to spot prey. When the class is writing a text that compares and contrasts, encourage them to use the weave planner – see Figure 12.6.

Figure 12.6 Weave Planner

Sequential text

Linear string

This kind of writing involves setting out a series of steps over time, one after the other, e.g., the steps in milking a cow. It could also help to plan a cause-effect structure, e.g., an earthquake causes the ground to move, which then causes buildings to collapse, and people to get hurt. Students can use the linear string planner to write about this kind of topic – see Figure 12.7.

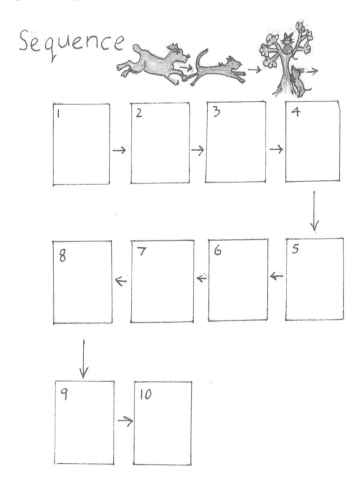

Figure 12.7 Linear String Planner

Problem-solution

This kind of writing involves a problem that has to be solved, e.g., a church is on the wrong side of the road – the solution is to move it to a better spot. Or, the problem might be that rats, cats, and hedgehogs are killing skinks (little lizards). The solution is to build a refuge for the skinks. Or, the problem might be that pupils miss the bus each morning because it is full. This has actually happened. A school bus was too full of other children and had to drive past students waiting to catch it. A solution for the children might be to provide them with a scooter or bike so they can get to school until the company can purchase more buses. Students writing about a problem-solution topic should use the planner in Figure 12.8.

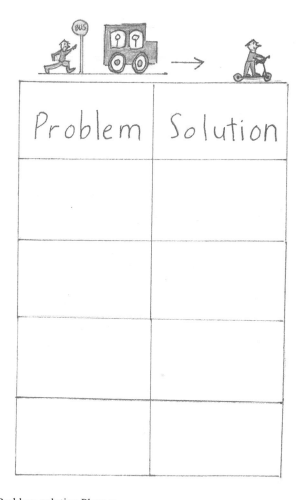

Figure 12.8 Problem-solution Planner

Persuasive text

Speech

In writing a persuasion text, such as a speech, the student has to consider the audience and predict how well the audience will receive their ideas. There are two factors to consider and find counter-arguments for when writing persuasion texts:

- Be aware that the audience might disagree with you
- Be aware that opinions will differ

Writing that uses a persuasion structure usually states a position (the claim) and then backs it up with several reasons to support the claim, e.g., to convince teachers and pupils that you should be the school captain. Or, to convince buyers to buy a product. Using a checklist can help the pupil with persuasion writing – see Table 12.3

Table 12.3 Student Checklist for a Persuasive Essay

Features I need	Check if you have these ✓
Title	
A hook (to grab the reader's attention)	
Reason 1	
Reason 2	
Reason 3	
Strong conclusion (a sentence or two)	

Debate

Writing with a debate structure involves persuasion. It has a "for and against" design – see the debate planner in Figure 12.9. Those debating a topic often give both sides of the argument but try to persuade the audience that their side has better arguments.

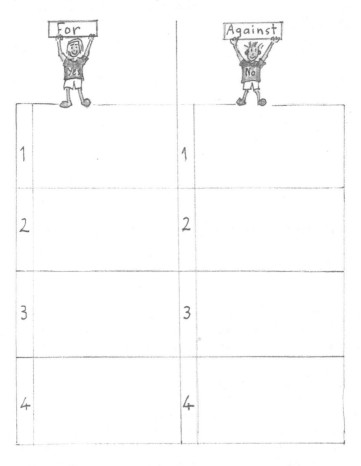

Figure 12.9 Debate Planner

12.6   Presentation of expository writing

Every piece of expository writing needs a strong beginning and end. Some elements of presentation also help, e.g., a title for the writing, indented paragraphs, and accurate spelling. The essay also needs to start with a hook to engage the readers to make them want to continue reading, e.g., "Did you know there are more than 900 million dogs in the world?" The essay should end with a conclusion that speaks to the reader, e.g., "I hope this has helped you to learn a lot more about dogs."

12.7   Beyond the first sentence – how to get started in writing

Sometimes all it takes to encourage pupils to start to write is to engage with them. Show interest in them as people and in their work and you have won them over. For example, one of us once visited a classroom with a trainee teacher who was sitting at the back of the class. The trainee did not want to bother the class at work, but we suggested they might want to sit with the pupils and engage with them, and encourage them to write. It would be more fun as well. Pupils do remember positivity, and the next time they see that teacher trainee, they are likely to wave to them and say hello. ☺

Some pupils might not know how to start their writing. They spend so much time thinking about what to write that they run out of time and hardly write any words. It may help to have ways to get them started faster, simple expressions like "keep going" – see Table 12.4.

Table 12.4 Ideas to Overcome "Writer's Block."

Problem	Solution
I can't think where to start.	Just start, write a few words, then a few more – soon you will be off to a great start.
I don't know what to write about.	Use your planner, it will guide you.
I don't know how to write a sentence.	Write two sentences. Choose the better one.
I'm afraid to write.	You write well. You can do it.

With older students, the teacher might ask them to break the task into chunks. Sometimes the topic seems too daunting to start. An eight-year-old pupil might want to write about their city or town but it seems overwhelming. The teacher might suggest narrowing the topic to just the main street of the town. If that is too much, focus on one building on that street, and if that is too much then focus on just one part of the building, e.g., the doorway or a window. The teacher is trying to encourage the student to break the task into chunks and build from there.

Simple structure reminders make a difference as well. Little reminders act as a guide to get started – be sure to have a title, open with a hook, indent each paragraph, use subheads to make the essay easier to read, finish with a conclusion that speaks to the reader. These are all important steps in writing that students need to know how to do well.

12.8   Conclusion

Teaching how to use text structure to compose effectively gives children not just writing tools but also a technical language to talk about their work. Imagine when parents ask their child about the story they wrote that day at school, they will be so impressed when their child tells them how they created a spooky setting to start the story, how they gave their characters personality and emotion, how they made sure there was a major problem the characters had to resolve, how their story had rising action and falling action, how there was a "complication" to the plot that put the reader on the edge of their seat, and how they put in a subtle "message" at the end. When children talk like this, using the language of writers, it is the beginning of being a writer.

Part V
Spelling

13 Spelling

What is it?

13.1 Introduction

Spelling has several faces to it. Spelling is the process of writing alphabetic characters (graphemes) in a sequence that corresponds to the sequence of phonemes in spoken words and matches conventional spelling as revealed in a dictionary. The beginner speller has to map the phonology of the spoken word onto print but at the same time capture its orthographic "spelling-print," that is, its correct spelling. Finally, the beginner speller has to consider the morpheme structure of the word, e.g., to spell the past tense ending always as -ed, no matter how it sounds. There is much to learn to spell well, but the teacher can help the student on this exciting journey.

Spelling matters. It can worry parents and children. In her book *Wild Things*, Sally Rippin (2022) wrote about her child and the impact that dyslexia had on their reading and writing progress at school. She wrote that parents need to get on top of issues like reading and spelling "before they hit grade three ... This is the age when kids start to notice that everyone around them is continuing to advance" (p. 244).

Difficulty with spelling negatively affects the quality of writing (Graham et al., 2011). If spelling is not accurate and automatic, it slows the writer down and uses up mental energy better needed for expressing ideas (Berninger, 1999).

This chapter will cover

- How well children spell
- Research on how children spell
- The first stages of spelling
- Teaching to spell simple consonant-vowel-consonant patterns, e.g., *cat*
- The "cipher" is the foundation
- Spelling Anglo-Saxon vowel sounds
- Spelling multi-syllable words

DOI: 10.4324/9781003130758-18

13.2   How well do eight-year-old children spell?

The spelling challenge for children in the early years of school is huge. By the time they are eight years of age, the expectation is that they can spell most words that they read and write.

This expectation is reached by some children but not all. In the 2023 NAPLAN spelling results (Australian Curriculum, Assessment and Reporting Authority [ACARA], n.d.), the test data for the country as a whole indicated that 11% of eight-year-olds, in Year 3 of school, had serious challenges in spelling and needed extra support – see Table 13.1. These children could only spell a small number of simple words. At first glance, this does not seem a large proportion of children, but it is worth noting the significant variability in the data. For children whose parents had a University degree only 4.5% needed additional support. For children whose parents did not complete senior secondary education, 30.6% needed additional support. Finally, for Indigenous children in very remote areas, 70.8% of these Year 3 children needed additional support.

What should we make of these data? A positive aspect is that the variance in the data helps teachers to see the bigger picture. They are a signal to think about how best to help all children to spell well. What is happening at the moment is working for many but not for some. We have to find a better way.

Table 13.1 NAPLAN Spelling Results for Year 3 Children (8 years 5 months).

	Total children	*Parent education – University degree*	*Parent education –Year 11 or below*	*Indigenous children in very remote areas*
Need additional support	11.1%	4.5%	30.6%	70.8
Developing	26.2%	20.9%	30.0%	16.9
Strong	44.1%	48.9%	29.6%	9.7
Exceeded	16.7%	24.4%	5.8%	0.7%

Note. Explanation of special categories: "Need additional support" means "can spell a few simple words." "Developing" means "can spell most simple words correctly." "Strong" means "can spell most common words correctly." "Exceeded" means "can spell many difficult words correctly."

13.3   What the research says about children's spelling

Studies of children's misspellings (Broc et al., 2021; Joshi et al., 2008) indicate that many misspellings fit into three categories:

1 Phonological – the word has some phonemes missing, e.g., *lump-lup*
2 Orthographic – some phonemes spelled incorrectly, e.g., *duck-dak*, *shirt-shert*
3 Morphemic – inflection incorrect, e.g., *jumped-jumpt*

Treiman (2017) suggested that children, at a certain point, start to teach them-selves to spell. She called it graphotactic learning, e.g., noticing that -

- Some consonant digraphs like *th* occur frequently – so *th* must be one sound, not two
- Double letters come after single vowels, e.g., *rubble* versus *trouble*
- Words starting with *w* often spell the /o/ sound as *a*, e.g., *was*, *watch*, and *wasp*.

13.4   The first stages of spelling – code and cipher

Some research studies indicate there are two stages in learning to spell. First there is the code stage, then there is the cipher stage (Gough, 1993). The code stage is when the child tries to remember the look of the word, the visual form of the word. The cipher stage is when the child follows the alphabetic principle that each successive grapheme in a written word corresponds to the same phoneme in the spoken word.

The two types of beginner spellers make different kinds of spelling errors. The cipher speller might misspell *tight* as *tiet*. The misspelling is phonologically cor-rect, i.e., sounds right. In contrast, the code speller might spell *meat* as *meta*. It does not sound right. They are trying to remember the look of the word.

The code speller is relying on memory for the visual form but to do this is to set yourself up for failure. There are too many words to remember how to spell this way. They are trying to remember all the letters, or relying on some distinctive cue or letter to remember words. At a certain point, many words start to look the same, e.g., we-went-wet. Code-cipher theory says that eventually the code begin-ner speller must change their ways and learn the cipher. Those who do change to cipher spelling will progress; those who do not will fall behind.

If children embrace the cipher, this will give a strong foundation for their spell-ing. On top of this foundation, they build accurate orthographic knowledge, i.e., knowledge of the correct spellings of words, both regular and irregular spellings. They are likely to remember the correct spelling much more easily if they know the cipher. When you think about it, the cipher speller will be able to spell even an irregular word because of the cipher. All they have to do is remember the irregular part of the word. Using cipher skills makes it easier to learn and store in memory the correct spelling.

When reading the research on teaching spelling to beginners, it does seem that the best way to start learning the cipher is with the 26 letter-sounds covered in Chapter 3, Figure 3.3. When children can fluently recognise and spell the 26 letter-sounds, they can progress to spelling words with single consonants and short vowel sounds (e.g., fan, sun) and then words with adjacent consonants (e.g., br-, cl-), and then consonant digraphs (e.g., ch, sh), and then to the long sound for single vowels, as in the split digraph rule. As they progress, the teacher can check progress by constructing simple worksheets where students practise the spelling patterns they have learned, e.g., fan, frog, kite, fish – see Figure 13.1.

Figure 13.1 Worksheet to Practice Basic Spelling Patterns

13.5   The importance of spelling by rule

A number of studies suggest that spelling by rule (i.e., using cipher knowledge) helps children to develop their spelling skills. Skilled spellers are more accurate when spelling regular words; developing spellers much less so (Gough & Walsh, 1991). Skilled spellers build on a foundation of spelling rules and use these to help them not just with regular spellings but with irregular spellings. This makes sense because even in irregular words, much of the word will be regular and only one section will be irregular.

How does the teacher help the class to learn the rules? It will not happen overnight, but it will be a lot easier if the teacher follows a scope and sequence. The first step is to focus on the spelling rules of Anglo-Saxon words. Later, teach the spelling rules that apply to Latin/French words. Finally, teach the spelling rules that apply to Greek-based words (Calfee & Associates, 1981).

In support of spelling rules, we taught 7-year-old children to use a small set of spelling rules (e.g., the *ai-ay* long vowel pattern, the *hop-hoping-hopping* doubling rule pattern) to learn words that we selected from published reading materials for that age group. Children improved their spelling. The rules helped them spell the words they learned in the lesson and the "rules" helped them to spell words they had not seen before (Dymock, 2019; Dymock & Nicholson, 2017). Teaching rules helps, it transfers to spelling of new words.

English is a complex mix of spellings from several major colonisers, the Anglo-Saxons, Romans, the French, the missionaries who brought the Latin Bible, and Renaissance scholars and scientists who borrowed many words from Greek to describe their inventions and discoveries. Children in the early years of school need to focus on Anglo-Saxon spellings, the bread-and-butter words of English. After that, children need to focus on the more sophisticated Romance (Latin/French) and Greek words prevalent in text material at the higher grade levels.

Anglo-Saxon words are the everyday words of English that feature in most children's reading material in the early years of school, ages 5–8. Romance (Latin/French) borrowed words feature in text material for older children, ages 9–10. Greek-based words, mostly content-specific words, are more prevalent in reading material for ages 11–12 and beyond.

Each layer has different spelling patterns as shown in Table 13.2. The Anglo-Saxon letter-sound patterns are often single consonant-vowel-consonant (e.g., *cat*), consonant digraphs (e.g., *shop*), single vowel with final e marker (e.g., *hat-hate*), r- and l-affected vowel sounds (e.g., *fur, walk*), and vowel digraphs (e.g., *seat*). Syllable patterns are mostly of the closed type, where the vowel sound is short, e.g., *magnet*. The next most common syllable pattern is the open type, where the vowel sound is long, e.g., *baker*.

In Anglo-Saxon spelling, morpheme patterns are evident in words that combine two base words, e.g., *raindrop* or a base word with a simple prefix and/or suffix, e.g., *like – **unlike** – **unlikely***. In the Romance layer of English, many words have a prefix – root word – suffix structure, e.g., ***pre**-script-**ion***. There are some new letter-sound patterns, e.g., ti = /sh/. In the Greek layer many words have a compound structure, e.g., ***geo-logy***. New letter-sound patterns include ch = /k/, ph = /f/, y = /i/.

Table 13.2 Examples of Spelling Patterns in Different Layers of English.

	Letter-sound patterns	Syllable patterns	Morpheme patterns
Anglo-Saxon	cat clock shop hat-hate fur seat	magnet baker	footstep raindrop like unlike unlikely
Romance (Latin, French)	disruption horrible excellent	inter- retro- -able	eruption prescription inscrutable
Greek	physics pharmacy	geo- chromo-	telescope chlorophyll psychology

13.6   Anglo-Saxon vowel sounds

As seen in the examples in Table 13.3, the long vowel sounds are a challenge for the beginner speller. For example, the student can spell the long /a/ vowel sound in several different ways, *ai*, *ay*, *a_e*, and *ei*. One helpful rule is to spell *ai* in the middle of the word, as in *sail*, and *ay* at the end of the word, as in *say*. Not commonly occurring but still worth learning are the ei and eigh spellings of the long vowel sound /a/. Some irregular spellings of the long /a/ sound include *ey* in *they*, *et* in *ballet*, and *ae* in *reggae*. With beginners, suggest teach *they* as a "tricky" word with an uncommon spelling of the long /a/.

Table 13.3 Multiple Ways to Spell Long Vowel Sound /a/.

Ways to spell long /a/ vowel sound	Examples	Spelling pattern
a_e	date came late cake	Split digraph (final e)
ai	sail main paid train	Vowel digraph (ai in the middle of word)
ay	say tray play hay	1-sound vowel digraph (ay at the end of word)
ei	reindeer vein	Vowel digraph
eigh	eight weigh	Vowel digraph
ey	they	Less common spelling of long /a/
aigh	straight	Only word like this
ae	reggae	Less common spelling of long /a/
et	ballet	Less common spelling of long /a/

When children make misspellings, the problem areas are often to do with the long vowel sounds, though there will be other issues as well, such as the spelling of morpheme endings (-ed) e.g., "A groop of boys and gerls war plauing football." The rules can help to correct some (but not all) of these misspellings, e.g., the child spelled the long /a/ vowel sound in "playing" as "au" but we could teach them to separate the base word and suffix "play-ing" and then use the rule that we normally spell the long /a/ sound as "ay" at the end of a base word like "play".

Table 13.4 shows the main spelling for Anglo-Saxon short and long vowel sounds. In the table, the short vowel sounds all have one regular spelling (except /e/ as in *head* and *bread*). In contrast, the long vowel sounds have two or more spellings. The "exception" spellings are words that do not occur very often but that children will need at some point to learn to spell. The tricky part of these exception words is usually the spelling of the vowel sound, e.g., short vowel sound /o/ in *was*, long vowel sound /a/ in *they*.

Henry (2010) suggests, particularly for vowel sounds, that the focus should be on the most common spelling patterns. If children are familiar with the most common spelling of vowel sounds as shown in Table 13.4, it will narrow down the possibilities and help them to make better choices when spelling.

Table 13.4 Spelling of Short and Long Vowel Sounds – What to Teach.

		Rule-based spelling				Exceptions
Short vowel	/a/	a – cat	-	-		plait
sounds	/e/	e – net	ea – bread	-		any, friend
	/i/	i – tin	-	-		gym, pretty
	/o/	o – dog	-	-		was, gone
	/u/	u – up	-	-		come
Long vowel	/a/	ai – rain	ay – hay	a/e – ate		they
sounds	/e/	ee – bee	ea – leaf	e/e – Eve	ie – thief	she, baby, key
	/i/	y – sky	igh – high	i/e – pine	ie – pie	wild,
	/o/	oa – oat	ow – tow	o/e – bone		no, toe
	/u/	ew – new	ou – soup	u/e – cube	oo – boo	blue, do, music
r-affected	/ar/	ar – car				fast, half
vowel	/er/	ur – fur	er – her	ir – sir		work
sounds	/or/	or – fork	au – haunt	aw – saw	al – talk	war
Other vowel	/ow/	ow – cow	ou – out			plough
sounds	/oi/	oi – oil	oy – toy			
	/oo/	oo – cook				put, could

13.7   Spelling multi-syllable words

In the early stages of teaching spelling, the teacher's focus is on spelling of one-syllable words, but when the teacher comes to multi-syllable words, they will need to explain that if multi-syllable words start with an open syllable, we use single vowels rather than vowel digraphs to spell the long vowel sound in such words – see Table 13.5.

Table 13.5 Spelling Multi-Syllable Words with Open Syllable Patterns.

Long vowel sound	Spelling	Example
/a/	a	ba/by, a/ble
/e/	e	de/duct, Pe/ter
/i/	i	pi/lot, tri/cycle
/o/	o	ro/bot, jo/king
/u/	u	tu/lip, cu/pid

In Chapter 3, we looked at the six syllable rules. It is worth thinking of these rules when spelling multi-syllable words, e.g., if the student at first thinks to spell *horrible* as *horrabull*, we should point out the rule about words ending in *-le* as in *cattle, jumble*, and *terrible*. We do not spell the suffix /ble/ as "bull." A better attempt for *horrible* will be to think of "horror" and "-ble."

13.8   Conclusion

The secret to accurate and fluent spelling is not necessarily working harder; it is about working smarter, and understanding the sound-letter rules. Morphology is also important and there are rules for analysing words in terms of their morphemic units, such as prefixes and suffixes. Knowing the "cipher", i.e., the letter-sound rules of English and how they relate to the history of English writing, is the foundation for spelling progress and success. Every house needs a strong foundation, and every spelling journey starts with the "cipher." As children learn the cipher, this equips them to know what fits the rules and what to learn as "exceptions" to the rules. The research on spelling indicates that the ability to spell irregular words is built on the ability to spell regular words. First teach the foundational skills of the cipher, then build on this to learn the exceptions. This is how to become skilled in spelling. The teacher and their pupils, together, can make success in spelling happen.

To teach spelling successfully, the teacher must win over their class of pupils to the idea that there is a rule-based system when spelling English words and it applies to all the words they come across in print, not just the ones they learn in class but in everything they read and write. The rules will help them. They do not have to memorise words by their "look". They can spell words phonologically – by sound. The rules will not enable them to spell every word correctly but they are the foundation and young spellers can build on this, and make adjustments for "exceptions". It will not happen overnight but in time it will ensure that their mental dictionary specifies the correct orthographic spellings of words. Spelling instruction that teaches the cipher rules of English in a systematic, step-by-step way, will ensure children's ability to spell well.

14 Assessing spelling

14.1 Introduction

A friend's child is four years old. The early childhood centre sent home a list of 25 high-frequency words ("sight words"). The instructions from school were that the child should practice reading and spelling the words. This seemed a tough call for the parents and the child. The child does not yet know all the alphabet names or sounds. The child told the parents, "I can read *I* and *daddy*." The words *I* and *dad* were on the list of 24. She pointed to *is* and said, "That's *I*." She could not find *daddy*.

The school is obviously well-intentioned. It is wonderful they are trying to give children a head start in literacy learning, but this is not the best way to learn to read and spell. It will not end well to memorise the landscape of whole words. Children need to learn to spell words by sound, phoneme by phoneme. It is not effective to memorise words by their visual "look." Too many words will look the same to them, words like *I* and *is*. It is better to spell words by their sounds and use spelling "rules."

This is why spelling assessment is so important to find out if children in the class are on the right track or on a road to nowhere. Are they spelling the right way? Assessment gives the teacher insight as to whether or not they will succeed or fail.

This chapter covers

- Standardised assessment of spelling
- Informal diagnostic assessment of spelling
- Case studies of spelling

14.2 Standardised measures

A standardised measure of spelling will give accurate data on children's current spelling level. For example, the Wide Range Achievement Test – Spelling (WRAT) normed in the US gives all sorts of helpful data, including stanine scores, standard scores, percentile scores, and an estimated grade level.

Teachers could use a published measure of spelling such as WRAT, but a speed bump is that such measures may require the user to have a specialist qualification in assessment. This is often the case for published, normed tests. For this reason,

DOI: 10.4324/9781003130758-19

a standardised measure of spelling may not be a realistic option for the classroom teacher to use unless the school has access to a trained assessor. Otherwise, the teacher needs to find another way.

One option is the Schonell Spelling Test (Schonell & Schonell, 1956). It is quite an old test, but it can give an approximate indicator of children's spelling achievement. Its norms cover the five-to-eight-year-old age range. In this test, the student spells each word as the teacher reads them aloud. The teacher can assess the whole class in one sitting. The test is easy to score and gives an approximate spelling age for each pupil. Prices vary. It may be available online, e.g., for further information see https://assessment.tki.org.nz/Assessment-tools-resources/Selecting-an-assessment-tool/Browse-assessment-tools/English/Spelling/Schonell-Essential-Spelling-List

14.3   Informal measures – diagnostic spelling test

A standardised measure will tell the teacher where the child is at in spelling but will not explain why or give insight as to what to do to help them progress. The teacher needs to use an informal, diagnostic measure.

An informal measure that we have found helpful in teaching is the Diagnostic Spelling Test (Chapman & Tunmer, 1995; Prochnow et al., 2013). It has high reliabilities, $r = .94$. It consists of 18 one-syllable words with rule-based spellings – see Table 14.1. Each student has an answer sheet – see Table 14.2. The words in the test are – *fat, fill, lump, pop, bank, side, hay, meat, kick, hot, pack, yell, van, duck, jail, bit, cake,* and *tight.* The teacher reads each word aloud, first on its own, then in a sentence, then on its own again as in the teacher's copy of the test. The student spells each word on their answer sheet. The teacher may assess one child, a group, or the whole class in one sitting.

Scoring. The maximum correct score is 18. There is also a "points" score for pre-conventional spelling. Each attempt receives a score between 0 and 4. The total possible number of points is 72. The points-scoring system is

4 – Correct spelling
3 – Sounds right but unconventional spelling, e.g., *kik* for *kick, fil* for *fill, sid* for *side*
2 – More than one phoneme correct but not all, e.g., *sd* for *side, lup* for *lump*
1 – The initial letter is correct, e.g., *f* for *fat*

On the student copy, record a score out of 4 points for each word in the test. Add up the scores for the words where the student gained the maximum score of 4. This is the score for words correct out of 18. Add up the points for all 18 words. This is the points score out of 72.

Benchmark score. There are no normed benchmarks for children aged 5–8 on this test, but informal data we collected from a group of 113 children who were six-to-seven-year-olds suggests a benchmark score of 9 out of 18 correct and 57 out of 72 points.

Table 14.1 Diagnostic Spelling Test – Teacher Copy.

	Say the word	Say it in a sentence	Say again
1	fat	My dog is too fat	fat
2	fill	Please fill my glass	fill
3	lump	He has a lump on his head	lump
4	pop	Don't pop the balloon	pop
5	bank	She put her money in the bank	bank
6	side	He painted the side of the house	side
7	hay	Cows like to eat hay	hay
8	meat	Dogs like to eat meat	meat
9	kick	She likes to kick the ball	kick
10	hot	It was a hot day	hot
11	pack	She put her book in the pack	pack
12	yell	Never yell in the classroom	yell
13	van	Father has a big van	van
14	duck	She gave the duck some bread	duck
15	jail	Robbers go to jail	jail
16	bit	The cat bit her finger	bit
17	cakc	The children ate some cakc	cake
18	tight	The shoe was too tight	tight

Total Correct ___/18
Total points ___/72

Note. Use of the test is with permission of Professor Emeritus James Chapman, Massey University.

Table 14.2 Student Record Form for Diagnostic Spelling Test.

Name _____
Date _____
Age _____
a b c d e f g h I j k l m n o p q r s t u v w x y z
1
2
3
4
5
6
7
8
9
10
11
12
13
14
15
16
17
18

14.4   Case studies – diagnostic spelling test

Case study 1

This pupil attempted all the words in the Diagnostic Spelling Test. The pupil was at the beginning stages of learning to spell and was able to spell the first sound for each word – see Figure 14.1. Although no words were spelled correctly, the student did score 14 points for phonemic spelling. They were able to spell the first sound of some words. The teacher can build on this. A starting plan for teaching would be to revise the 26 letter-sounds – see Figure 3.3 in Chapter 3, first practising spelling the individual letter-sounds, and then spelling simple consonant-short vowel-consonant patterns on the sidebar of the chart. Then use the other lists of spelling patterns from Chapter 3. Spell the sidebar words, explain the rules behind them, and have students put them into context, spelling the words in sentences.

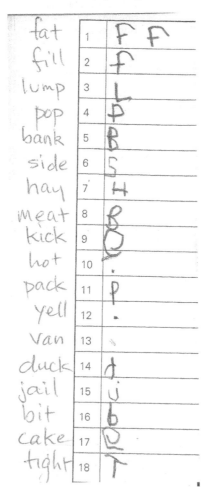

Figure 14.1 Case Study 1 – Diagnostic Spelling Test

Case study 2

This student scored 10 words correct and gained 60 points – see Table 14.3. What does this tell the teacher besides that they scored 56% correct? The student spelled correctly most of the consonant-short vowel-consonant patterns (except "bit"). Some long vowel spellings were on the right track but not the conventional spelling – *jail-jill, hay-hey, tight-tiet.* Some split digraph spellings were not split, *side-sied, cake-caek.* With this student, the teaching plan would be a brief revision of consonant-short vowel-consonant patterns to ensure the /u/ and /i/ short vowel sound spellings words are secure. Then move to more advanced spelling patterns, e.g., r- and l-affected vowel sounds and vowel digraph patterns – see the 21 week spelling programme in Chapter 15.

Table 14.3 Analysis of Results Case Study 2.

	Test word	Pupil response	Points	Problem
1	fat	✓	4	
2	pop	✓	4	
3	hot	✓	4	
4	van	✓	4	
5	bit	bite	2	short vowel sound i
6	pack	✓	4	
7	duck	✓	4	
8	kick	✓	4	
9	lump	lamp	2	short vowel sound u
10	bank	✓	4	
11	hay	hey	3	vowel digraph *ay*
12	meat	✓	4	
13	jail	Jill	2	vowel digraph *ai*
14	fill	full	2	l-affected vowel -ill
15	yell	✓	4	
16	cake	caek	3	split digraph a/e
17	side	sied	3	split digraph i/e
18	tight	tiet	3	vowel digraph *igh*
Total words = 10/18			Total points – 60/72	

Case study 3

This pupil scored 8 words correct and 55 points – see Table 14.4. What does this tell the teacher apart from that the child scored 44% correct? The student did seem to be spelling by sound and encoded the right number of phonemes for words but not always the correct spellings, e.g., *cake-cack* and *tight-tite.* The student spelled all consonant-short vowel-consonant patterns correctly. In terms of a teaching program, the teacher could skip those words and focus on words with r- and l-affected vowel sounds and vowel digraph patterns – see 21 week spelling programme in Chapter 15.

Table 14.4 Analysis of Results Case Study 3.

	Test word	Pupil response	Points	Problem
1	fat	✓	4	
2	pop	✓	4	
3	hot	✓	4	
4	van	✓	4	
5	bit	✓	4	
6	pack	pak	3	final -*ck*
7	duck	dack	2	short vowel *u*
8	kick	✓	4	
9	lump	lamp	2	short vowel *u*
10	bank	bace	2	cluster -*nk*
11	hay	✓	4	
12	meat	meet	3	vowel digraph *ea*
13	jail	jall	2	vowel digraph *ai*
14	fill	full	2	l-affected vowel -*ill*
15	yell	yall	2	l-affected vowel -*ell*
16	cake	cack	2	split digraph *a/e*
17	side	✓	4	ake pattern
18	tight	tite	3	vowel digraph *igh*
Total correct = 8/18			Total points = 55/72	

Case study 4

This pupil scored 3 out of 18 correct and 39 out of 72 points for phonemic spelling – see Figure 14.2 and Table 14.5. What does this tell the teacher apart from the child achieving a score of 17% correct? One reason for the lower points score for phonemic spelling was because the student wrote some letter-sounds in the wrong order, e.g., *fill* as *fla*. It could be that they have not yet fully clicked onto the alphabetic principle that we spell words phoneme by phoneme. An initial teaching lesson might focus on phonemic spelling. One activity is "turtle talk," where you teach the pupil to stretch out the sounds in spoken words, count the sounds, and say each sound separately, e.g., the sounds in /hill/ are /h-i-ll/; the sounds in /vet/ are /v-e-t/. This will be a check that they can "hear" the sounds in the right order. Another idea is to write the word on the board, then point to each phoneme, e.g., f-igh-t.

A teaching suggestion is to go back to the 26 letter-sounds chart and revise sounds that were confused on the test – see Figure 3.3, Chapter 3. Using the chart, revise the spellings of the /u/, /i/, and /e/ short vowel sounds, revise the spelling of the final /k/ sound for the word *duck,* and the spelling of initial consonant /y/ in *yes*. Practice spelling the sample words on the sidebar of the 26 letter-sounds chart. When the child is fluent in spelling the sample words, move to consonant cluster words with short vowel sounds – see Figure 15.6

in Chapter 15 – and revise final consonant clusters such as -lk (milk), -nt (tent), -mp (lamp), -nd (hand), and -nk (bunk). Finally, teach split digraphs, l-affected vowel sounds, and one-sound vowel digraphs – see spelling programme in Chapter 15.

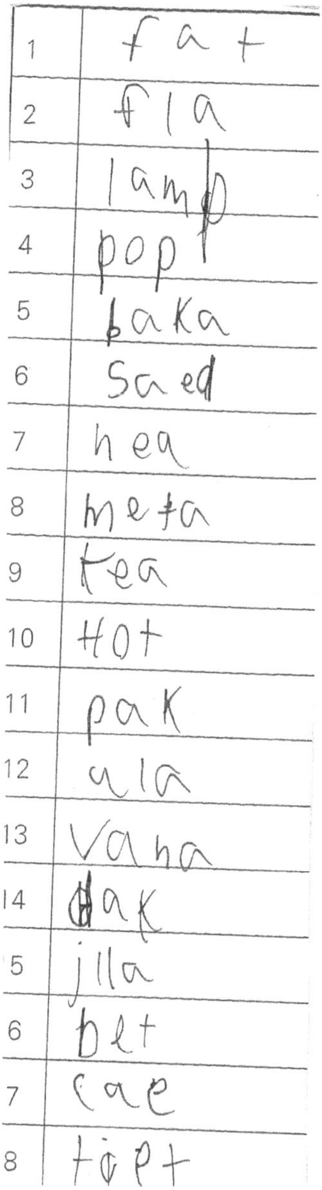

1	f a t
2	f l a
3	l a m p
4	p o p
5	b a k a
6	s a e d
7	h e a
8	m e t a
9	f e a
10	H o t
11	p a k
12	u l a
13	v a h a
14	d a k
5	j l l a
6	b e t
7	c a e
8	t o p t

Figure 14.2 Case Study 4 – Diagnostic Spelling Test

Table 14.5 Analysis of Results Case Study 4.

	Test word	Pupil response	Points	Problem
1	fat	✓	4	
2	pop	✓	4	
3	hot	✓	4	
4	van	vana	2	added extra letter
5	bit	bet	2	short vowel *i*
6	pack	pak	3	final -*ck*
7	duck	dak	2	final -*ck*
8	kick	kea	1	short vowel *i* final -*ck*
9	lump	lamp	2	short vowel *u*
10	bank	baca	2	cluster -*nk*
11	hay	hea	1	vowel digraph *ay*
12	meat	meta	2	vowel digraph *ea*
13	jail	jlla	2	vowel digraph *ai*
14	fill	fla	2	l-affected vowel -*ill*
15	yell	ula	0	consonant /y/ l-affected vowel -*ell*
16	cake	cae	1	split digraph *a-e* final /k/
17	side	saed	2	split digraph i-e
18	tight	tiet	3	vowel digraph *igh*
Total correct = 3/18			Total points = 39/72	

14.5   Conclusion

The ability to use the alphabetic principle when spelling is the foundation for ef-fective spelling. Using the alphabetic principle to spell words is not enough in itself because there are so many irregular words that break the "rules," but it is the foundation to build on.

It is so important for children to learn the alphabetic principle and learn to spell the many words in English that follow regular "rules." Once students can do this, they will build on this foundation and add to their growing mental dic-tionary the many "exception" words that make up the quirks and curiosities of the amazing English spelling system.

15   Teaching spelling

15.1   Introduction

Children seem to like learning the academic language of spelling. In one study, we asked 7-year-old children for feedback on what they liked about the lessons. A number of them wrote, not always with correct spelling, that they liked learning about "selabls" (syllables), the *"rabt roll" (rabbit rule)*, the "dubling roll" (doubling rule), *"majik e" (magic e)*, *"vowles,"* *"a e i o u,"* "captalls" (capitals), and *"comers"* (commas). One wrote that spelling lessons helped them to improve their writing, "My writing has gotten a bit faster." These comments suggest that children like learning how to spell by rule.

Yet sometimes we make spelling into a chore that children do not like. In many schools, spelling is a list of 15–20 words that children take home on Monday and take a spelling test on the same words on Friday. Is this an effective way to learn? It may be for some but many parents tend to think not, that it causes stress and sadness at home as their children grapple with a task that is too hard for them.

This chapter covers

- Research on teaching spelling
- A programme for teaching spelling
- Teaching handwriting
- Teaching punctuation

15.2   What makes a top speller?

At first glance, English spelling seems to be an awful mess. Too many words do not seem to fit any rules. Spelling mistakes seem to crop up everywhere, e.g., the local newspaper recently reported that a council bus sign read "bus sopt."

On the other hand, some children are fantastic spellers. Anyone who has watched the movie Spellbound knows that in the U.S. spelling competitions are a national pastime. The ultimate prize is to win the Scripps National Spelling Bee. Students from all over the country compete. In 1980, the winning word was "sarcophagus"

DOI: 10.4324/9781003130758-20

but in recent years the words given to contestants seem a lot harder, e.g., "apodyterium" (Kronholtz, 2010). The winner in 2021 was 14-year-old Zaila Avant-garde. She became the first African-American to win the bee. To win the competition she had to spell "murraya," a type of tropical tree. She asked about the origin of the word (from Latin) before she spelled it. On her way to winning, she had to spell "querimonious" and "solidungulate." Earlier that evening, she hesitated over "nepeta," which means herb, but spelled it correctly.

When Zaila was asked about how she learned so many words, she said she practised 7 hours each day. The message that comes from events like the Scripps National Spelling Bee is that to be a skilled speller requires much deliberate study and practice, and when reading the reports of these spelling bees, what also comes across is a love of spelling among these students.

The top spellers had achieved remarkable skill. How did they do it? They said that they did an enormous amount of practice and study and that they studied the origins of words and the history of English spelling. They had obviously learned the rules of spelling so well that they could spell almost anything.

15.3   The research on learning to spell

How do we teach children to spell well? How do children become top spellers? The research says that children will make more progress if we teach spelling explicitly and in a structured and systematic way (Graham & Santangelo, 2014; Pan et al., 2021). Explicit teaching involves the teaching of spelling rules, and following a scope and sequence that covers the rules from simple to complex – see Table 15.1 and Figure 15.5.

In one study (Dymock & Nicholson, 2017), we wanted to see if explicit teaching of spelling rules was better than rote learning of words. In that study, 55 children, all seven-year-olds, were randomly assigned to rules training, rote learning, or no training. The "rules" group learned spelling rules, e.g., the *ai-ay* rule, as in *sail-say*. The rule is to spell *ai* in the middle of the word and *ay* at the end. The "rote" group practised writing the same words several times in isolation and in a sentence, but they were not told the words followed a rule. A control group did not learn the words explicitly but they read with the teacher a story that had those words in it, they discussed the book's storyline, and did punctuation exercises. The results showed that the rules group and the rote group both learned the test words better than did the control group. The important thing, however, was that the rules group transferred their learning to spelling of different words that followed those same spelling rules. For words not seen before, their spelling was better than the other two groups. This study gave support to teaching spelling rules.

The teaching of rules can also help spelling of advanced words. In one study, eight-year-olds learned to spell Latin-based words (Butyniec-Thomas & Woloshyn, 1997). They learned the base word-suffix pattern, e.g., *educate* (drop the e) and add *-ion*, *-ing*, or *-ed*. They learned how to spell words like *information*, *education, vacation, location, relation, direction, formation, election,* and *correction.* The results showed much improvement for the trained group. Although there was no control group in the study, their results do suggest that this is a practical technique for teachers to teach spelling of words with a similar morpheme structure, that is, with prefixes and suffixes. With younger children, such as five-to-six-year-olds, the teacher could use less complex but similar base word-suffix patterns, e.g., plural (-s, -es), present and past tense (-ing, -ed), and comparison (-er, -est) for words like *bush-bushes, stamp-stamped-stamping,* and *loud-louder-loudest.*

How much time each day should teachers give to spelling? In one classic study, the researcher tested children in many schools across the US, using a 50-word spelling test. The researcher asked teachers how much time they spent teaching spelling each day. The researcher compared children's spelling progress across the schools noting how much time they spent on spelling, and concluded that 15 minutes of teaching a day was sufficient for children to make reasonable progress (Rice, 1897; Ayres, 1912). This was an old study but more recent survey data suggest that U.S. teachers seem to spend about the same amount of time each day, on average18 minutes (Graham et al., 2008). However, other studies in Australia and England have found that teachers of younger children spend more time than that (Daffern & Critten, 2019; Dockrell et al., 2016; Esposito et al., 2022).

15.4   Developing a structured spelling programme

An explicit and structured spelling programme is one that follows a coherent scope and sequence – see Table 15.1 and Figure 15.5. The scope and sequence in Table 15.1 starts with short vowel sounds and single consonants and finishes with long vowel sounds and multi-syllable words. The first words children learn to spell in Table 15.1 are vowel-consonant (VC) and consonant-vowel-consonant (CVC) patterns. The final column in Table 15.1 has lesson ideas, based on the spelling programme in the Appendix to this chapter – plus charts from previous chapters.

Additional rules – useful details to know include:

1 -ff, -ss, -ll, and -zz at the end of a word, e.g., *off, mess, hill,* and *buzz*
2 -ck at the end of a word after a short vowel, e.g., *duck*
3 -tch in the middle or end of a word after a short vowel sound, e.g., *catch* and *kitchen*
4 -dge after a short vowel sound, e.g., badge and judge
5 -ve if the word ends in *v*, e.g., *love, give, have,* and *live*
6 -*ce* for /s/ after long vowel sound e.g., race and ice
7 "rabbit rule" – double the consonant after a short vowel sound, e.g., butter

Table 15.1 Scope and Sequence for Teaching Spelling Ages 5–8

Scope and sequence	Spelling patterns	Test words	Lesson ideas
VC and CVC words with short vowel sounds	s a t p i n m d g o c k ck e u r h b f l j v w x y z q	at, sat, pat in, pin, tin on, cat, dog egg, up, sock hat, bag, fan jug, van, web, box yes, zip, quiz	Spelling programme weeks 1–7. Figures 3.2, 3.3, 13.1
Consonant clusters with short vowel sounds	**Initial** – bl br cl cr dr fl fr gl gr pl pr sc sk sm sl sn sp st sw tr tw scr spl spr squ str shr thr **Final** – -ft -mp -nt -lk	black, crab, flag pram, slug, skip tram, twins, scrub shrub, tent, milk	Spelling programme week 8. Figure 15.6
Consonant digraphs with short vowel sounds	ch, sh, th, ng, wh	chip, shop, then/thick, song, when	Spelling programme week 9. Figure 3.4
Split digraph CVCe (or "magic e") words with long vowel sounds	a-e, e-e, i-e, o-e, u-e	a: mad made e: pet Pete i: bit bite o: hop hope u: cut cute	Spelling programme weeks 10–14. Figures 3.5, 15.2
Long vowel sounds, (vowel digraphs)	ai-ay ee-ea-ie ie-igh oa-ow oo-ou-ue-ew	rain, ray bee, tea, thief pie, night boat, tow boo, soup, glue, new	Weeks 10–14, Figures 3.9 to 3.11
Other vowel sounds	ou-ow oi-oy oo	out, cow toil, toy book, cook, look	Weeks 19–21, Figures 3.10-3.12, 15.7
r- and l-affected vowel sounds	ar er-ur-ir or-au-al-aw air-ear-ure	car fern, surf, bird fork, haunt, ball, saw hair, fear, cure	Weeks 15–18, Figures 3.6 to 3.8
Simple suffixes and the doubling rule ("rabbit rule")	-s, -ed, -ing	hop, hops, hopped, hopping	-
Compound words		uphill, railroad, kingfish	-
Multi-syllable words	**Syllable types-** closed open split digraph r-affected vowel digraph -le	mag/net ro/bot con/crete var/nish fif/teen jug/gle	Figure 3.14

15.5   Teaching spelling at ages 5–6 and 6–8

At ages 5–6, start with VC and CVC spellings – see the chapter appendix weeks 1–7. The focus is on single consonants and short vowel sounds, e.g., week 3 words with /g/ sound include *gap, gag, gig, nag, sag, gas, pig,* and *dig.* Then move to words with consonant digraphs – see week 8, e.g., chick, chop, chin, chug, check, such, and chip. The next step would be to spell words that start and end with consonant clusters (adjacent consonants) – see week 9, e.g., slug and tent.

At ages 6–8, children will probably be skilful in spelling CVC words with short vowel sounds and words with consonant digraphs and clusters. The teacher can then move to the spelling of one-syllable words with long vowel sounds. They can also move to r-affected vowel sounds. Initially teach just one spelling pattern for each vowel sound – see the chart in Figure 15.1. This keeps it simple. Later, once children know these patterns, teach the other long vowel sounds – see chapter appendix weeks 10–21.

The teacher can construct spelling quizzes to help teach some of the spelling rules. An example of a spelling quiz for the split digraph rule is in Figure 15.2. The student has to circle the correct spelling. The teacher could make up other quizzes.

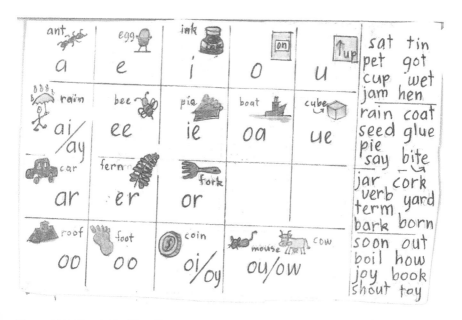

Figure 15.1 Simple Spelling Chart

a -e i o u

1		ap	ape
2		hate	hat
3		mad	made
4		home	hom
5		pine	pin
6		pin	pine
7		not	note
8		tube	tub
9		fir	fire

Figure 15.2 Quiz – Split Digraph Rule

15.6   Lesson plan – example

Imagine you have a class of five-year-olds. It is week 1. You need to teach the class to spell words with the letters s-a-t-p. How would you do this? What will your plan be? Table 15.2 is a template that the teacher can use to teach spelling.

Table 15.2 A Sketch of a Spelling Lesson for SATP Words.

Opening – purpose of lesson	Handwriting
Hello everyone, today we will write some words. Now, what are the sounds of these letters (T writes **s a t p**)? The first sound is … Next one? Next one? Last one is … Good job!	I want you to practice writing the letters **s a t p** in your books. Finger space between each letter. Start with s – from the top, wind around and down and up again, etc. Good job!
Spelling	**Phonemic awareness**
(T writes *at* on board). What does that say? /at/. Now, spell **at** in your books. Good job.	What is first sound in /at/ – /a/, what is last sound – /t/? What are the two sounds in /at/? Can you say /at/ slowly, /a-t/?
More practice	**Sentence**
(T writes **sat**). What does that say? Now, spell **sat** in your books. (T writes **tap**). What does that say? /tap/. Now, spell **tap** in your books. Good job. (T writes **pat**). What does that say? Spell **pat** in your book. Good job.	(T writes **Pat sat at tap**). Read the sentence for me. Write the sentence in your book.
Morphology	**End of lesson**
(T adds s to **tap** – what does that say). Yes, it says taps – taps is the plural of tap. The **s** means there is more than one tap.	What sounds did we learn to spell today? **s-a-t-p** What sentence did we write? **Pat sat at tap**. Well done. Thank you.

15.7 Teaching handwriting

The aim of teaching handwriting is to teach each child to write legibly, fluently, and with speed. Charts in Figures 15.3 and 15.4 show the lowercase and uppercase letters with some dotted examples that students can copy. It is important to practise as much as possible until handwriting starts to look neat and consistent.

Berninger (2012) defined handwriting as "the use of the hand to produce units of written language – single letters, written words, sentences, and text – to express ideas and thinking" (p. 28). The research indicates that handwriting is important for spelling – neatness counts.

Writing by hand somehow acts as a glue to help students remember the shape of letters and the correct spellings of words, more than does keyboarding. Studying uppercase and lowercase script, tracing and copying, writing letters from memory, and then comparing them with the correct forms, these activities can build not only handwriting skills but also letter-sound knowledge which is crucial for reading and writing (James & Berninger, 2019).

Figure 15.3 Handwriting – Lowercase Letters

Figure 15.4 Handwriting – Uppercase Letters

15.8   Teaching punctuation

Punctuation and spelling go hand in hand. It is important to teach some basic rules about punctuation. For beginners the first basic rule is to start the sentence with a capital letter and end with a full stop. Remembering to capitalise the names of people, places, and days of the week is also important. Table 15.3 has 10 rules to teach (Samson, 2015).

Table 15.3 Ten Punctuation Marks for Beginners.

Punctuation marks	Notation	Examples
Capital letter – The first word in the sentence and the first letter for names, places, months, and days of the week.	ABC	They all wanted to help. Jane, Auckland, January, Monday
Full stops – Always at the end of the sentence.	.	We all giggled.
Question mark – Only if you ask a question. Put at the end of the sentence.	?	Is it a treasure chest?
Exclamation mark – An exclamation mark shows the speaker is saying something with force or loudly. Put at the end of the sentence.	!	Ahoy there! Oh no!
Comma – Use when there is a slight pause in the sentence.	,	I ate apples, pears, and plums today. On Sunday, we had chicken for lunch.
Speech marks – Remember speech marks only go around words spoken. Speech marks have to enclose the entire sentence spoken.	" "	"Go home." Mum said, "Hello."
Apostrophe – Used for abbreviations. Used for possession. The apostrophe is not necessary to indicate plurals, e.g., trees.	'	can't Ernie's cat.
Hyphen – Adds more to the sentence.	-	There were peanuts and a carrot – but no sandwiches.
Parentheses – Can go around some words in the sentence.	( )	The workers at the factory (especially Ernie) were pleased to see him.
Ellipsis – Some words are left out …	…	She hid behind the bushes and waited and waited …

Note. At the end of a sentence, you can have a full stop, a question mark, or an exclamation mark – but only one of these.

Quiz – Take a quick punctuation test ☺
(Answers at the end)

1 Which of these sentences has incorrect punctuation?

   a. This question isn't easy
   b. Is this the right answer?
   c. "I hope I get this one right," she said to herself.

2 Which of these sentences has incorrect punctuation?

   a. "That's John's apple!" he shouted.
   b. All the shop's are closed on Christmas day.
   c. My cat's name is very silly.

Answers – 1a (the sentence has no full stop), 2b ("shops" is plural, does not need apostrophe)

15.9 Advanced spelling rules – structural analysis – morphology

At some point, usually later in the spelling programme, at the six- to eight-year level, students need to tackle morpheme structure. Morphemes are the smallest meaningful units of speech. Morphemes are not intuitively obvious. They can be very small, e.g., the plural suffix s, or can be a whole word, e.g., salamander. The thing is that they are one meaningful unit.

Morphemes include prefixes, suffixes, and root words. Prefixes are morphemes at the start of a word (e.g., re- means to repeat or do again, as in re-open and re-write). Suffixes are found at the end of words and usually indicate things like part of speech, tense, or plurality (e.g., adding s to the end of words indicates the plural form, as in cats, dogs, and bushes; adding -ed to the end of a word indicates past tense). Morpheme knowledge can help the speller to decide the correct spelling – is it *trees* or *treez*? The morpheme rule is that if it is a plural, then we spell *tree* as *trees*. Using the rule, the child can work out to spell the plural of *socks* with an *s*. If the word ends in /ks/, but is not a plural, then do not add *s*, and instead use x, or xe (e.g., fox, axe).

For borrowed words from Latin, where the suffix has a /sh/ sound, we spell the /sh/ sound as ti, si, ci – e.g., *action, tension, delicious.*

Should we spell -ion or -ian? The difference between the spelling of -ion and -ian is that -ian refers to someone who does something (e.g., *electrician, musician, magician*).

For borrowed words from Greek, there are some new spellings to learn, e.g., ch for /k/, ph for /f/, y for /i/ – *chemist, phone, gym.*

More suffix patterns

- *s* for plural, e.g., *cats, dogs*
- ed for past tense, e.g., *sacked, robbed*
- ing for present tense, e.g., *jumping*
- er for person, e.g., *jumper*
- -er/-est for comparison, e.g., *bigger, biggest*

15.10 Conclusion

Students sometimes make spelling errors that they do not need to make if they know the kinds of spelling rules we have talked about in this chapter. We can teach rules that will enable them to write words correctly, not *traen* or *trayn* but *train*. The skilled speller follows the advice suggested in this chapter, e.g.,

1 They segment spoken words into all their phonemes.
2 They use sound-to-print rules (e.g., /ow/ at the end of a word is usually *ow*).
3 They practise – not a big panic session before the test.
4 They use graphotactic learning (e.g., /o/ after *w* is *a* as in *wand* and *watch*).
5 They look for morphemes in words – prefixes, suffixes, root words.
6 They know the different spellings of Latin words (e.g., /sh/ sound in *nation* is *ti*).
7 They know the different Greek spellings (ch- *chemist*, ph- *phrase*, y- *myth*).

APPENDIX

Spelling programme

The words in all the spelling lists below only use letter-sounds that the class has already covered in previous weeks, e.g., the *inmd* words in week 2 only use the letters *satp* and inmd. The spelling eel in Figure 15.5 shows the scope and sequence that the lists follow in weeks 1–21.

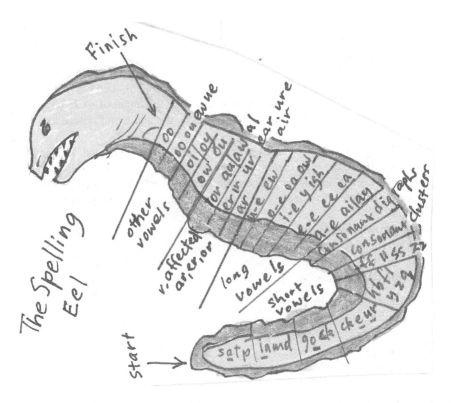

Figure 15.5 Spelling Eel – Scope and Sequence

Week 1 – satp

Check that pupils can say the sound correctly of each letter *s-a-t-p*. Check they can **read** words made from the letters, *at*, *sat*, *tap*, and *pat*. Demonstrate how to spell those words, say the word, segment the phonemes, and spell each phoneme letter on the board. Ask them to spell the words in their notebooks.

s	sat
a	at
t	tap
p	pat

Week 2 – i n m d

i	it, sit, sat, pit, tip, pip, sip
n	in, nip, pan, pin, tin, tan, nap
m	am, man, mat, map, Pam, Tim, Sam
d	dad, sad, dim, dip, din, did, Sid, and

Week 3 – g o c k

g	gap, gag, gig, nag, sag, gas, pig, dig
o	on, not, pot, top, dog, pop, got
c	can, cot, cop, cap, cat, cod
k	kid, kit, Kim, Ken

Week 4 – ck e u r

ck	kick, sock, sack, dock, pick, sick, pack, ticket, pocket
e	get, pet, ten, net, pen, peg, met, men, neck
u	up, mum, run, mug, cup, sun, tuck, mud, sunset
r	rim, rip, ram, rat, rag, rug, rot, rocket, carrot

Week 5 – h b f l

h	hat, had, him, hot, hut, hop, hum, hit, hug
b	bag, but, big, back, bet, bad, bed, bud, beg, bug, bun, bus, Ben, bat, bit, bucket, rabbit
f	fan, fat, fit, fin, fun, fig, fog, puff, huff, cuff, if, off,
l	log, lap, let, leg, lot, lit, bell, fill, doll, tell, sell, Bill, gull, laptop

Week 6 – j v w x

j	jug, jam, Jill, jet, jog, Jack, Jen, jet-lag, jacket
v	van, vat, vet, Vic, velvet
w	web, will, win, wag, wig, wax, cobweb
x	fox, mix, fix, box, tax, six

Week 7 – y z q

y	yap, yes, yet, yell, yum
z	zip, Zak, buzz, jazz, zigzag
q	quick, quiz, quit, quack

Week 8 – clusters (adjacent consonants)

Children need to practise spelling with consonant clusters (CCVC, CVCC, and CCVCC). The clusters are not new consonant sounds. All these adjacent consonants have regular consonant sounds. Some examples of cluster spellings are in the spelling quiz Figure 15.6. The quiz words are – *skip, pram, frog, drum, flag, slug, crab, tram, grub, plug, clock, steps, squint, black, twins, lamp, swing, strum, scrub, tent, milk, hand, gift,* and *trunk.*

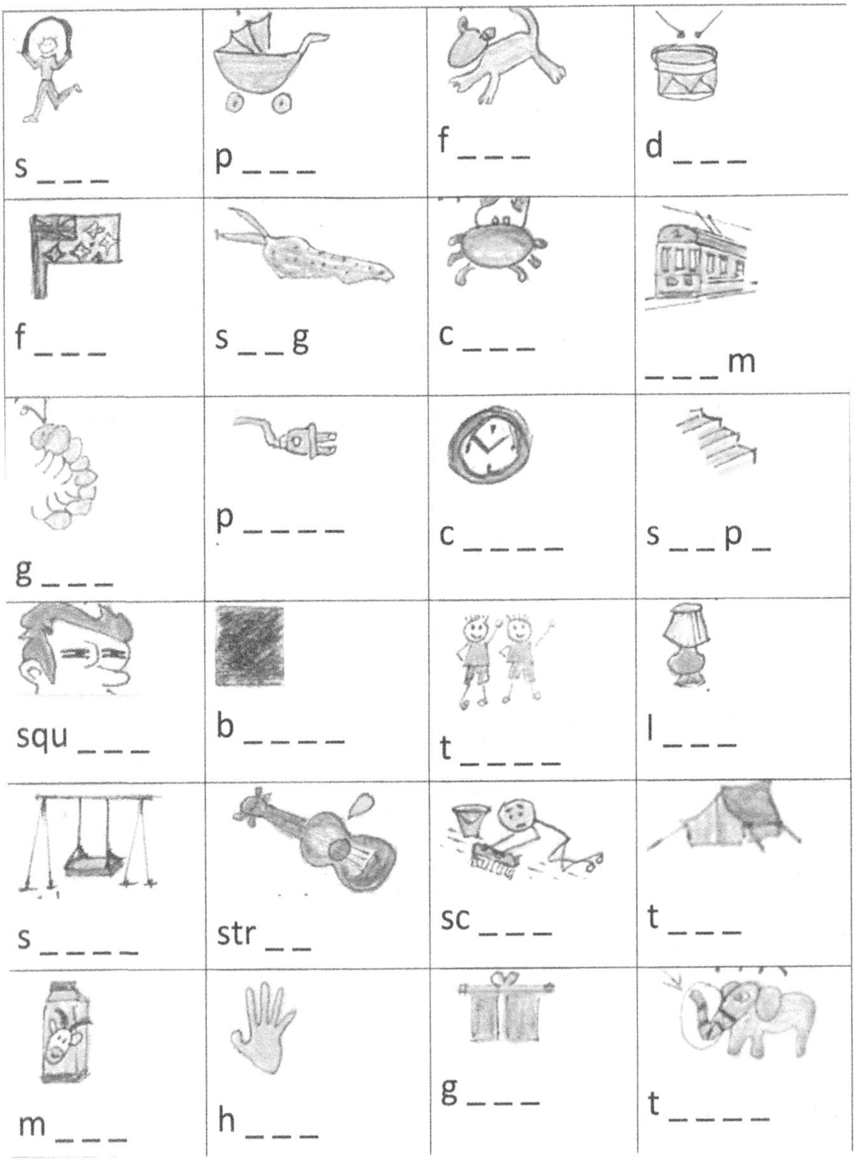

s _ _ _	p _ _ _	f _ _ _	d _ _ _
f _ _ _	s _ _ g	c _ _ _	_ _ _ m
g _ _ _	p _ _ _ _	c _ _ _ _	s _ _ p _
squ _ _ _	b _ _ _ _	t _ _ _ _	l _ _ _
s _ _ _ _	str _ _	sc _ _ _	t _ _ _
m _ _ _	h _ _ _	g _ _ _	t _ _ _ _

Figure 15.6 Spelling Quiz for Consonant Clusters

Week 9 – ch sh th ng – consonant digraphs

T – Morning, class. The consonant digraphs are new sounds. The scribes in the old days added h to some letters because their Anglo-Saxon language had more sounds than available letters (that were from the Roman alphabet). Teacher can mention that *th* has a strong and weak sound. Teacher can mention that we spell *ch* at the start of the word and *tch* at the end. Teacher can mention that for words from the English language, *-ng* is always at the end of the word.

Teacher demonstrates either on the whiteboard or with magnetic letters. Initially, give three to four examples – e.g., *chick, ship, the/thin,* and *song.*

ch	chick, chop, chin, chug, check, hutch, chip, chill, hatch, witch
sh	ship, shop, shed, shell, fish, shock, cash, bash, hush, rush
th	them, then, that, this
	moth, thin, thick, cloth, math
ng	song, ring, rang, hang, wing, rung, king, long, sing

Possible dictation exercise using ch sh th ng:

I sang a song in the fish shop.
The fish shop had hot chips.
The ship is at the dock.
The dog had chops.
The cat had chicken.

Week 10 – /a/ long vowel sound as in bake, *with three patterns: a...e, ai, and ay*

There are three common ways to spell the long /a/ – ai, ay, and a_e (split digraph).

1 Teach the split digraph rule. Give a contrasting example, e.g., at-ate to show how the rule works, showing how it changes the short vowel sound to its long sound.
2 The ai/ay rule. Teach that words with ai often end with n or l, e.g., sail and rain. Spell ai in the middle of the word and ay at the end.

Initially, demonstrate how to spell with a few examples – e.g., *train, hay,* and *gate.* Use other words in the lists to test for transfer.

ai	sail, main, tail, rain, bait, wait, hail, pain, aim
ay	day, way, may, hay, say, play, tray
a_e	came, same, take, safe, snake

Note to teacher: Exceptions – ey (they*)* and ea (*break*)

Week 11 – /e/ long vowel sound, as in bee, *which has three main patterns, ee, ea, and e...e*

Focus on three main ways to spell the long /e/ – ee, ea, and e_e (split digraph).

1 Review the split digraph rule. Gave a contrast example, e.g., pet-Pete to show how the rule works, showing how it changes the short vowel sound to its long sound.
2 The ee/ea pattern. There is no easy way to decide which way to spell /e/.

Other ways to spell /e/ long vowel sound are y (baby), ey (key), and ie (thief) – can be taught later in the programme. Demonstrate with a few example words – e.g., *tree, leaf,* and *Pete.*

ee	see, feel, weep, feet, jeep, seem, meet, week, deep, keep
ea	sea, team, each, heat, cream, speak
e_e	Eve, Pete

Exceptions for long /e/ include ay (*quay*), eo (people), and oe (*phoenix*). Explain that *we, me, he, she,* and *be* are the only words spelled like this – and they are high-frequency words.

Week 12 – /i/ long vowel sound – three main patterns, ie, igh, and i_e

T – The three main ways to spell the long /i/ sound are as follows:
ie – only a small number of words, like *pie, lie, tie*
igh – usually followed by a t – as in tight, fight
i_e – split digraph or final e rule, e.g., side

Demonstrate how to spell some examples – e.g., *bike, night,* and *pie.* Use other words in the lists to test for transfer of the rule, e.g., slide, tight, and tie.

i_e	bike, like, ride, slide, white, pride
igh	night, high, sigh, light, might, right, sight, fight, tight
ie	pie, lie, tie

Note – Exceptions to the rule – I (high-frequency word), eye, find, buy, and wild.

Week 13 – /o/ sound – three main patterns: o...e, oa, ow

T – Morning, class – The three main ways to spell the long /o/ vowel sound are as follows:
o_e – final e rule
oa – in middle of word
ow – as in the word *tow* (usually the long /o/ sound is spelled ow at the end of word).

Demonstrate how to spell some of the words in the list below. Segment the sounds while writing on the board – e.g., h-o-me, g-oa-t, and t-ow.

o_e	home, those, hope, woke, hose
oa	goat, coat, load, loaf, road, soap, oak, toad, foal, boat
ow	tow, snow, blow, own, grow, show

Note to teacher: Tricky spellings of /o/ include – no (high-frequency word), toe, sew, and dough

Week 14 – /oo/ vowel sound as in room

T – The three main ways to spell the long /oo/ sound are – the split digraph pattern *u_e* (*cube*), *oo* (*zoo*), and *ew* (*few*). Initially, demonstrate how to spell three to four examples – e.g., *moon*, *cube*, and *screw*.

oo	too, zoo, boot, zoom, cool, food, root, moon, roof
u_e	rule, June, rude, tube, tune
ew	few, grew, flew, drew, screw, threw

Note to teacher: Exception spellings of /oo/ include – to, two, and music

Week 15 – /ar/ sound as in car

T – Today, we learn to spell the /ar/ sound. There is only one way to spell it – "ar." Demonstrate some examples – e.g., park and barn. Segment the sounds, e.g., b-ar-n. Then give other words in the list to check for transfer of the rule.

ar	car, bar, far, arm, farm, barn, yard, bark, card, cart, hard, jar, park, scar, mark

Note to teacher: Tricky spellings of /ar/ include – half, laugh, bath

Week 16 – /or/ sound as in corn, core, haul, law

Teacher says, "Today, we study the spelling of the /or/ sound." The teacher explains that the main ways to spell /or/ sound are:

or – usually in middle of word (except *or* and *for*)
ore – normally end of the word
au – in middle of word
aw – normally end of word
-al – as in fall and chalk.

Demonstrate spelling with examples from the word list below – either on the whiteboard or with magnetic letters – e.g., corn, score, saw. Note the /or/ spelling in *walk, chalk, talk.*

or	for, fork, cord, cork, sort, born, worn, fort, torn, sport, storm
ore	score, before, wore, shore
au	haul, haunt, fraud
aw	draw, saw, law, straw, yawn, craw
al	talk, walk, wall

Note to teacher: Exception spellings of /or/ include – war, roar

Week 17 – /er/ sound, as in her, sir, fur, has three main patterns

T – Some common ways to spell /er/ sound are – ur (fur), ir (sir), and er (her). Demonstrate some examples – e.g., surf, bird, and fern.

ur	fur, burn, urn, burp, curl, hurt, surf, turn, church, turnip, curd, purr
ir	girl, bird, dirt, firm, shirt, first, third
er	These "er" words have a stressed /er/ sound – fern, term, her, herd, berm These "er" words have an unstressed /er/ sound, called a "schwa" sound – und*er*, bett*er*, wint*er*

Note to teacher: Tricky spellings of /er/ include – work, earth, and were (high-frequency word)

Week 18 – /air, ear, ure/ – just these patterns

T – There are other r-affected vowel sounds – *air (chair)*, *ear* (spear), and -ure (picture). Demonstrate how to spell some examples – e.g., chair, fear, cure.

air	hair, fair, pair, chair
ear	ear, dear, fear, hear, gear, near, year, rear, beard
ure	pure, cure, manure, picture

Week 19 – /ow/ as in cow, has two main patterns, ou, ow

There are two main ways to spell the /ow/ sound – ou and ow. Demonstrate some examples – e.g., town and ground.

1 Teach to segment the sounds before spelling the words, e.g., m-ou-se.
2 Remind the class to spell ow at the end of the word.
3 Give a quiz to decide the correct spelling, e.g., h__se, fr__n, cl__n, c__.

ow	cow, now, down, owl, how, pow, town, towel, brown, growl
ou	out, loud, mouth, round, sound, ground, shout

Note to teacher: Exception to the rule – "ough" for /ow/ sound as in *plough*.

Week 20 – /oi/ sound, as in toy and oil

T – There are the two main ways to spell /oi/ – oi is in the middle of the word and oy is usually at the end of the word. Demonstrate how to spell some examples – e.g., oil and boy.

oi	oil, boil, coin, coil, join, soil, toil, poison, foil
oy	toy, boy, soy, Roy

Note to teacher: No exceptions to this rule.

Week 21 – /oo/ sound as in "cook"

T – There is only one way to spell /oo/ as in *cook*. Spell it as *oo*. Demonstrate some examples – e.g., book and crook. To give the class some practice in reading and spelling *oo* words, try the worksheet in Figure 15.7.

oo	look, foot, cook, good, book, took, wood, wool, hook, hood

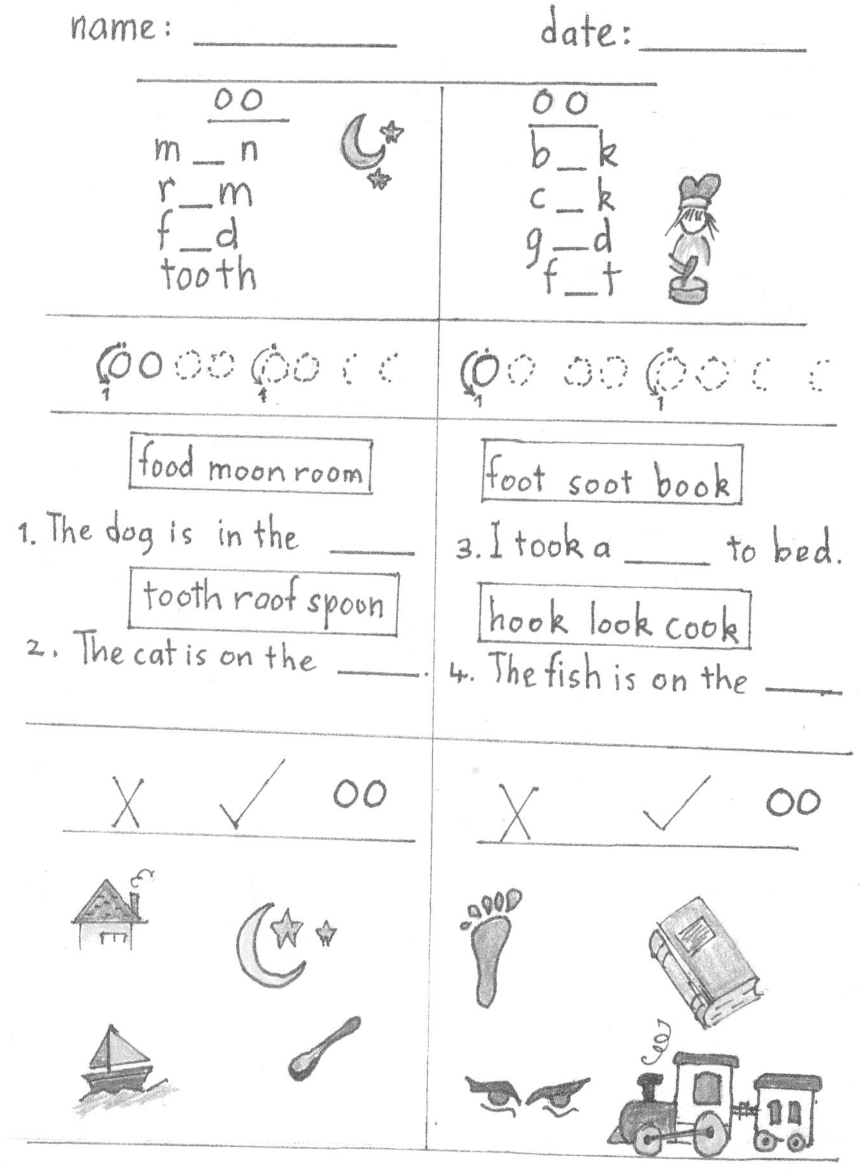

name: _____   date: _____

O O m _ n r _ m f _ d tooth	O O b _ k c _ k g _ d f _ t
((O O OO ((O ((	((O OO OO ((O ((
food moon room 1. The dog is in the ____ tooth roof spoon 2. The cat is on the ____	foot soot book 3. I took a ____ to bed. hook look cook 4. The fish is on the ____
X ✓ OO	X ✓ OO

Figure 15.7 Worksheet – Two Sounds of OO in Moon and Cook

Part VI
Planning to Teach

16 Countdown to teaching

16.1 Introduction

This book is a practical guide to teaching literacy, but to get the most out of it, the teacher needs to start planning well ahead of meeting the class for the first time. It may seem like overkill, but it is good to plan ahead. As the saying goes, try to "win at the starting line" which means to take action early in order to achieve success. Think about the school's literacy goals for the term, the students you will have, the state of the classroom, and the resources needed. Think about the teaching routine you will have. The class needs to know what they are doing and why they are doing it. No surprises. Planning and organisation is key. Confusion will never end well. The wise teacher only teaches one thing at a time, avoids creating a mishmash, does not try to teach everything at once but gives separate lessons on decoding, handwriting, spelling, vocabulary, comprehension, and writing. As the saying goes, keep it simple.

Teach one thing at a time and do it well. Avoid jumble. Every lesson must be organised with an opening, a middle, and a close. In the opening, say, "Today we are going to ...." In the middle, teach something new, e.g., "Look at this chart ...." In the close, say, "So today we learned about ...."

This chapter will cover

- Months ahead
- Weeks ahead
- Meeting the class for the first time
- Good behaviour strategies

16.2 Three months ahead

Start thinking about the class three months ahead. Here are some suggestions. Does the school have specific goals and objectives? What goals will parents have? What goals will children in your class have? What do you want students to learn? Your teaching goals can be in rough form and be revised later. Having goals clarifies thinking. Find out how many students are in the class. Check the school's achievement data. What are the reading and writing abilities of students? What are their social and cultural backgrounds? Do any students have special needs – what are they?

DOI: 10.4324/9781003130758-22

Check resources – Find out what instructional readers are available for this class. Is there an up to date series of graded, modern decodable books for beginners such as Sunshine Phonics Decodables series and Little Learners Love Literacy.

Make copies of the teaching charts that we covered in this book, e.g., the 26 letter-sounds chart in Figure 3.3. Laminate them or put them on PowerPoint to put on the walls, to show to the class. Do children have personal workbooks to write in?

Visit your classroom – is there enough (any) seating? Is there technology? Is it working? Do you have internet access? Take a photo of the room. How can you make the room work for you? It helps if you feel comfortable teaching in it.

16.3   Two months before school starts

Decide on the scope and sequence for instruction. Students and parents need to know where they are going in decoding, spelling, reading comprehension, and writing. You have to think about the scope and sequence you will follow for the year and how to plan each topic hour by hour, day by day. Should you give homework? In many homes, the weekly spelling test is a source of great stress for parents and children, especially if the words are too hard, if they are a random list of unrelated patterns with no consistent "rules" to help with spelling. The research on homework for reading and writing is equivocal. If the child has to take a book home, or a list of spelling words, make sure they know how to read the book and spell the words extremely well. They need to take home things that will make mum and dad proud. Do not send home things they cannot understand or will struggle with.

16.4   One month ahead – how will you teach?

The key to good teaching is **routine and simplicity**. No surprises. Every lesson follows the same format. If you are teaching decoding skills, start with a warm-up of something you taught the day or week before. Follow the same plan each time. Use the same charts. If the lesson is new, get the class ready for it; say that there is something new today. Do not throw in a new rule or new topic out of the blue. Simplicity is essential. Do not try to do too much at once. The child's brain can only handle two or three ideas at a time.

Another key is **coherence**. Teach only one thing at a time, and teach it in a coherent way, e.g., if you teach the beginning Set 1 letters "satp" in Figure 3.3, only ask the class to spell words that have "satp" in them. The teaching should always move from the known to the unknown, not vice versa. Build on what the class know, not on what they do not know.

Otherwise, it is a recipe for confusion. Build on what you did yesterday and the day before. Teach in increments, not too much at once. If something is tricky, say so. Explain why. Never give the class new words to spell with letters they have never seen before. Have a teaching plan, follow a scope and sequence, and start from the foundations, not from the roof. Each piece fits together in synchrony, builds on the other. Do not make it up as you go. If it is on the internet, be suspicious; there is so much snake oil out there. Only teach the best that is thought and said, that is backed by evidence, and that comes from experts and reputable sources.

Use **formal language** to teach literacy; do not shy away from the academic terms. Children need to know about the technical language of reading and writing. Then they can talk about these subjects with you and others, discuss what they are learning, ask questions, and delve further. If they know the technical terms of reading and writing, such as "consonants, vowels, digraphs, syllables, narrative, expository, introduction, conclusion", and so on, they can communicate with you in a clear way. In decoding lessons, for example, talk to the class about technical things like phonemes, vowel and consonant sounds, and digraphs – explain what the terms mean. Handwriting, talk about uppercase and lowercase, letter sounds and letter names. In lessons on comprehension, talk about setting, characters and plots of narrative texts, and webs, weaves, and sequence structures for expository texts. Vocabulary – talk about synonyms, attributes, features, and examples. Grammar – talk about subject and predicate. Punctuation – talk about capital letters and commas. Of course, we should avoid getting too carried away. These terms are just the tools of teaching literacy – they are not literacy. Going overboard with technical language was made fun of in a humorous newspaper article written for parents (O'Neill, 2016):

> Do you know what a split digraph is? It sounds like a painful muscle tear that DIY dads incur trying to put up a curtain rail. Well, it's not that. A split digraph, as my daughter (just turned six) explained to me recently, is when the "ee" or "ue" sound in a word is separated by a consonant.

Try to use **direct teaching**. Do not expect children to learn to read simply by reading them a book or a poem. Some may see the light, but most will not. Teach children directly and systematically how to decode and spell. Follow a scope and sequence.

Try to use mixed ability grouping for literacy lessons. Some studies suggest that dividing children into higher and lower ability groups may have negative Matthew effects, i.e., the "rich get richer and the poor get poorer" (Bolick & Rogowsky, 2016; Patrick, 2020). A suggestion is to avoid splitting the class into ability groups based on reading and writing levels, e.g., monkeys, tigers, elephants, etc. Instead, try every day to teach the whole class at once for most of the time. There is nothing wrong with the whole class reading the same book or doing the same spelling quiz together but we do not have to divide the class into ability groups. Sometimes, in the hurly-burly of a lesson, children working in small groups can be an oasis of quiet, as pupils complete tasks. But it is more inclusive if they all do the same task. It does not seem fair to have different activities for skilled readers and developing readers. If children all work together, it will still be effective. The skilled readers and writers will always do well. Encourage them to help the developing readers and writers. This builds social skills that are very important. It is a positive aspect of well-being to help others.

Teachers should "consider ways to ensure that students within the lowest reading groups receive equal access to rigorous instruction and materials." (Patrick, 2020, p. 631) We have seen many examples where this does not happen, where the lowest group does less rigorous activities, e.g., practising 10 sight words and reading a very simple book, while the highest group does more rigorous activities, e.g., reading a more sophisticated book and discussing plot and theme. The teacher is unwittingly creating a "rich get richer and the poor get poorer" situation. There is no reason why the whole class cannot work together, do the same curriculum, follow the same scope and sequence, work together, help each other, and praise each other's work. One or two simple words of encouragement from a peer can work magic, e.g., "You wrote a good story, Junior."

16.5   Two weeks ahead

Make lesson plans – see the sample lessons in Tables 16.1–16.3. The plans can be sketchy at first, and you can add detail later, but they will show the big picture of what you are trying to achieve in a week or term and will link into the scope and sequence of decoding and spelling lessons outlined in this book.

Checklist for a good lesson plan

✓ Explain the lesson plan to the class
✓ Warm-up, review previous lesson, write up the day and date and children write this in their workbooks. In a beginner class, in a decoding lesson, start with a very familiar task like reciting the sound of each letter in the alphabet chart (see Figure 3.3.). Then review a short list of tricky letter-sounds (Figure 2.2). Then show the class where they are up to on their scope and sequence chart and explain what will be the next learning task for them (see Figure 2.1),
✓ Opening of lesson – explain the goal of the lesson
✓ Closing – review – write down on the board what goals the class completed in the lesson

By all means supplement your decoding lessons with decodable books so children can practise the decoding rules, e.g., vowel digraphs, or comprehension topics they have learned, e.g., characters, plot. We have used titles from Sunshine Phonics Decodables series and Little Learners Love Literacy, but please look around for other publisher titles that may fit the rules you are teaching.

If you do not have decodable books in your classroom, you could create your own sentences or stories. The lesson plans below have some light-hearted stories and poetry that we made up using the words covered in decoding charts in Figures 3.3 to 3.12.

Table 16.1 Beginner Class – Year 1, Week 1.

Time	Topics	Monday	Tuesday	Wednesday	Thursday	Friday
9–9.45	Decoding	satp	satp	inmd	inmd	Review
9.45–10.30	Reading	Pat sat.	Pat sat at tap.	Pam sips at tap.	Sid sips at tap.	
			Morning Interval			
11–11.45	Handwriting	satp	satp	inmd	inmd	Review
11.45–12.30	Spelling	at, sat, pat, tap, sap	at, sat, pat, tap, sap	mat, sad, mad, tin, sip, pat, pan	sad, mad, tin, sip, pat, pan	
			Lunch Time			

Table 16.2 Lesson Plans for Year 2, Week 1.

Time	Topics	Monday	Tuesday	Wednesday	Thursday	Friday
9–9.45	Decoding	ch-sh	ch-sh	th-ng	th-ng	Review
9.45–10.30	Reading – e.g., made-up poem					

The fish shop had chips. Which chips? Hot chips. Yum. The fish shop had chops. Which chops? Hot chops. The fish shop had chicken. Which chicken? The fish shop had hot chicken. Yum. I sang. I sang a song. I sang a song in the shop. Which shop? The fish shop.

Morning Interval

Time	Topics	Monday	Tuesday	Wednesday	Thursday	Friday
11–11.45	Spelling	ch – chick chug check chip chicken	sh – ship shop, shed shell fish	th – them then th -thick moth with	ng – song ring rang king wing	Review
11.45–12.30	Writing, e.g., 10 minute story	prompt word: chicken	prompt word: fish	prompt word: moth	prompt word: king	Review

Lunch Time

Table 16.3 Lesson Plans for Year 3, Week 1.

Time	Topics	Monday	Tuesday	Wednesday	Thursday	Friday
Prior to 9:00 a.m. – The teacher works at her desk with one or two children to revise skills						
9–9.45	Decoding	ai-ay rain, hay, sail, train, tray	ee weed, seen, beep, feet, sheep	oa boat, road, soap, goat, float	oi-oy boil, soy, join, coin, toy	Review
9.45–10.30	Reading (made-up sentences)	The **rain** in **Spain** fell **mainly** on the **plain.**	The **sheep** in Spain fell mainly on the **jeep.**	The **goat** in Spain fell mainly on the **boat.**	The **oil** in Spain fell mainly on the **soil**.	Review

Reading (made-up story) **Max at the Beach**

Max woke up in his bed made of hay. He looked at the fern tree out in the garden. He saw a black bird sitting on a branch. He saw a leaf on the tree. The bird sang, "Good morning Max, time to rise and shine." Max cooked up some bread and pie and ate the lot. He milked the cow. He gave his dog a bone. He fed the cat. It was a good day for a bike ride but he had to put oil in the wheels to stop them squeaking. As he rode down the street, he went by the haunted house and the tow truck. He saw a cow on the road. Oh no, he forgot his lunch. He stopped at a shop to get a loaf of bread and a meat pie. "It will fill me up until I get home." When he got to the beach, he saw a sailing ship and a whale in the surf. Max had a fun day.

(*Continued*)

Table 16.3 (Continued)

Time	Topics	Monday	Tuesday	Wednesday	Thursday	Friday
	Comprehension	Who was the main character in the story? (Max.) What was the setting? (It was morning, the bird was singing, Max's bed, the street, the beach.) What was the first problem in the story? (Bike wheels squeaking.) The solution was? (Max put oil on them.) What was the next problem in the story? (Max forgot his lunch.) The solution was? (Max got bread and a meat pie from the shop.) What was the theme of the story? (Going for a bike ride is fun.)				
			Morning Interval			
11–11.45	Spelling	ai-ay sail, mail, rain, play, tray	ee feet, jeep, seem, deep, keep	oa goat, oats, load, loaf, road	oi-oy toil, coin, boil, toy, boy	Review
11.45–12.30	Writing – use 3 promptwords– 10 minute story	train, snail, tray	jeep, feet, keep	road, goat, oats	oil, boy, coin	Review
	Vocabulary	What is a tray?	What is a jeep?	What are oats?	What is toil?	Review
			Lunch Time			

16.6   One week ahead

Send out an email to parents welcoming their children to the class. Invite them to introduce themselves.

16.7   Meeting the class for the first time

This will be an exciting but anxious time for children – and you. The golden rule for the teacher is always be positive that you want them to do well and to have a happy time.

Things to try

- Have children introduce themselves, say their name, what they did in the vacation.
- Explain the daily routine, how each day will work, what they will do. Write a list on the whiteboard.
- Explain class rules
  - We sit nicely on the mat
  - We do not talk when the teacher is talking
  - No running in the classroom
  - We look after each other
  - We look after our things
- Explain what homework they need to do each night (if any).

16.8   Planning for good behaviour

Praise

Use behaviour specific praise, e.g., "I liked the way you read the alphabet sounds," "Good job," "I liked the way you read the story," "Well done," "I like the way you are sitting so nicely."

Calm

Try to correct misbehavior calmly and quickly, focusing on de-escalation rather than reprimand. Some students will need time out to calm down. Reiterate the class rules. The teacher has to adapt to the situation. In some classrooms it will only take a few words to get the class on track but in other classrooms it will be much more difficult. Try to use behavior specific praise, e.g. "I like the way everyone is sitting quietly." Praise when the class quiets down, or when a disruptive pupil calms down and re-joins the group.

Reduce task difficulty

Research suggests that classroom behavior will be better if the teacher makes sure that students read easier text material. In a classic study, the researcher found a negative correlation between pupil performance and text difficulty (Jorgenson, 1977). In other words, when text material was too difficult to read and understand, classroom behavior got worse. In contrast, when material was easier, behavior improved, as did children's comprehension of text and their creativity. This seems counterintuitive but in some ways it makes sense that when the literacy task is above children's ability levels, they are more likely to become frustrated. The teaching implication is that our pupils are more likely to engage with our teaching and be better behaved if the reading material is easy for them to read. There is no need for children to read material that is too hard. This is not good teaching. If it is too hard for them to read, and you definitely feel that it is important, then read it to them. If we give children reading material that is easier for them to read, where they will succeed, classroom behavior will improve. The classroom will be a happier place.

Rewards

Give points for good conduct. The class gets points for sitting up straight, being in their seat, attempting the lesson, not shouting, or being disruptive. If they get ten points, they get a small reward such as a sticker, five minutes of free time, or simply some teacher praise like "good job." The only caution is do not take off points for misbehaviour – students will think it unfair.

Choices

Choice helps in some cases. Give the class a choice of activities. If the task involves two things, write the tasks on a chart or whiteboard, then let the students choose which one they would like to do first.

Breaks

Sometimes, to settle the class, it helps to take mini-breaks, e.g., simple movement activities such as actions to go with a song.

Engagement

Try to encourage total engagement so everyone is on task at the same time. If children are not on task, try the every pupil response (EPR) technique where the whole class engages with the activity, e.g., the teacher gives the class a worksheet, then gives EPR directions for everyone to circle the word that starts with CH, underline the word that ends in NG, read the word that ends with a final e, spell the word on the worksheet that means "something you walk on" (e.g., feet, road). These activities encourage everyone to engage with the task.

16.9 Conclusion

The key to teaching literacy is planning, simplicity, teaching one thing at a time, avoiding jumble, using formal language, and using direct and systematic teaching every day, for most of the time. Planning and organisation will unlock the door to a successful teaching term. Start planning at least three months ahead of meeting the class for the first time. Routine is the key when you meet the class every day. Always start with an easy task that everyone can do. No surprises. Organisation. Be positive. Never raise your voice. Always be calm. Enjoy each lesson. If you are happy, the class will be happy. Have fun!

References

Australian Curriculum, Assessment and Reporting Authority [ACARA] (n.d.). *NA-PLAN national results*. Retrieved June 4, 2024, https://www.acara.edu.au/reporting/national-report-on-schooling-in-australia/naplan-national-results

Anderson, R. (1978). Schema-directed processes in language comprehension. In A. M. Lesgold, J. W. Pellegrino, S. D. Fokkema, & R. Glaser (Eds.), *Cognitive psychology and instruction* (pp. 67–82). Plenum.

Ayres, L. P. (1912). Measuring educational processes through educational tests. *The School Review, 20*(5), 300–309.

Baynton, M. (1995, May). *Birth of a book. A difficult labour from conception to delivery.* [Paper presentation]. Twenty-First New Zealand Conference on Reading, Invercargill, New Zealand.

Beattie, K. (2021). *Andrew and Sue make a kite.* Wendy Pye Publishing Ltd.

Berninger, V. (1999). Coordinating transcription and text generation in working memory during composing: Automatic and constructive processes. *Learning Disability Quarterly, 22*(2), 99–112. https://doi.org/10.2307/1511269

Berninger, V. W. (2012). Strengthening the mind's eye. The case for continued handwriting instruction in the 21st century. *Principal, 91*(5), 28–31.

Berninger, V. W., Vaughan, K., Abbott, R. D., Begay, K., Coleman, K. B., Curtin, G., Hawkins, M., & Graham, S. (2002). Teaching spelling and composition alone and together. *Journal of Educational Psychology, 94*, 291–304. https://doi.org/10.1037/0022-0663.94.2.291

Biemiller, A., & Slonim, N. (2001). Estimating root word vocabulary growth in normative and advantaged populations: Evidence for a common sequence of vocabulary acquisition. *Journal of Educational Psychology, 93*(3), 498–520. https://doi.org/10.1037/0022-0663.93.3.498

Block, C. C., & Parris, S. R. (Eds.). (2008). *Comprehension instruction: Research-based best practices* (2nd ed.). Guilford Press.

Block, C. C., & Pressley, M. (Eds.). (2002). *Comprehension instruction: Research-based best practices.* Guilford Press.

Block, C. C., & Pressley, M. (2003). Best Practices in literacy instruction. In L. M. Morrow, L. B. Gambrell, & M. Pressley (Eds.), *Best practices in literacy instruction* (2nd ed., pp. 111–126). Guilford Press.

Bolick, K. N., & Rogowsky, B. A. (2016). Ability grouping is on the rise but should it be? *Journal of Education and Human Development, 5*(2), 40–51.

Brenner, D., & McQuirk, A. (2019). A snapshot of writing in elementary teacher preparation programs. *The New Educator, 15*(1), 18–29. https://doi.org/10.1080/1547688X.2018.1427291

Broc, L., Joye, N., Dockrell, J. E., & Olive, T. (2021). Capturing the nature of spelling errors in developmental language disorder: A scoping review. *Language, Speech, and Hearing Services in Schools, 52*(4), 1127–1140. https://doi.org/10.1044/2021_LSHSS-20-00086

Brown, D. (2008). Using a modified version of the vocabulary knowledge scale to aid vocabulary development. *The Language Teacher, 32*(12), 15–17.

Brown, K. J., Patrick, K. C., Fields, M. K., & Craig, G. T. (2021). Phonological awareness materials in Utah kindergartens: A case study in the science of reading. *Reading Research Quarterly, 56*(S1), S249–S272. https://doi.org/10.1002/rrq.386

Bryant, N. D. (1975). *Test of Basic Decoding Skills* [Unpublished manuscript]. Teachers College, Columbia University, New York.

Buckingham, M., & Goodall, A. (2019). The feedback fallacy. *Harvard Business Review, 97*(2), 92–101.

Butyniec-Thomas, J., & Woloshyn, V. E. (1997). The effects of explicit-strategy and whole-language instruction on students' spelling ability. *Journal of Experimental Education, 65*(4), 293–302. https://doi.org/10.1080/00220973.1997.10806605

Calet, N., Lopez-Reyes, R., & Jiminez-Fernandez, G. (2020). Do reading comprehension assessments result in the same reading profile? A study of Spanish primary school children. *Journal of Research in Reading, 43*(1), 98–115. https://doi.org/10.1111/1467-9817.12292

Calfee, R. C. (1984). Applying cognitive psychology to educational practice: The mind of the reading teacher. *Annals of Dyslexia, 34*, 219–240.

Calfee, R. C. (1991). What schools can do to improve literacy instruction. In B. Means, C. Chelemer, & M. S. Knapp (Eds.), *Teaching advanced skills to at-risk students* (pp. 176–203). Jossey-Bass.

Calfee, R. C. (2005). The exploration of English orthography. In T. R. Trabasso, J. P. Sabatini, D. W. Massaro, & R. C. Calfee (Eds.), *From orthography to pedagogy* (pp. 1–20). Lawrence Erlbaum.

Calfee, R. C., & Associates. (1981). *The book: Components of reading instruction.* [Unpublished manuscript]. School of Education, Stanford University.

Calfee, R. C., & Drum, P. (1978). Learning to read: Theory, research and practice. *Curriculum Inquiry, 8*(3), 193–294. https://doi.org/10.1080/03626784.1978.11075571

Calfee, R. C., & Drum, P. (1986). Research on teaching reading. In M. Wittrock (Ed.), *Handbook of research on teaching* (pp. 804–849). Macmillan.

Calfee, R. C., & Patrick, C. L. (1995). *Teach our children well: Bringing K–12 education into the 21st century.* Stanford Alumni Association.

Cali, D., & Balducci, M. (2022). *Too many pigs and one big bad wolf: A counting story.* Tundra Books.

Cao, Y., & Kim, Y. G. (2021). Is retelling a valid measure of reading comprehension. *Educational Research Review, 32*:100375, 1–25. https://doi.org/10.1016/j.edurev.2020.100375

Carver, R. (1987). Should reading comprehension skills be taught? In J. E. Readence & R. S., Baldwin (Eds.), *Research in literacy: Merging perspectives* (pp. 115–126). Thirty-sixth Yearbook of the National Reading Conference. National Reading Conference.

Castle, J. M., Riach, J., & Nicholson, T. (1994). Getting off to a better start in reading and spelling: The effects of phonemic awareness instruction within a whole language program. *Journal of Educational Psychology, 86*(3), 350–359. https://doi.org/10.1037/0022-0663.86.3.350

Castles, A., Rastle, K., & Nation, K. (2018). Ending the reading wars: Reading acquisition from novice to expert. *Psychological Science in the Public Interest, 19*(1), 5–51. https://doi.org/10.1177/1529100618772271

Catts, H. W. (2021). Rethinking how to promote reading comprehension. *American Educator, 45*(4), 26–33, 40.

Cervetti, G. N., Fitzgerald, M. S., Hiebert, E. F., & Hebert, M. (2023). Meta-analysis examining the impact of vocabulary instruction on vocabulary knowledge and skill. *Reading Psychology, 44*(6), 672–709. https://doi.org/10.1080/02702711.2023.2179146

Chapman, J. W., & Tunmer, W. E. (1995). Development of young children's reading self-concepts: An examination of emerging subcomponents and their relationship with reading achievement. *Journal of Educational Psychology, 87,* 154–167.

Connelly, V., O'Rourke, L., & Sumner, E. (2019). How being a poor speller can seriously limit your talent as a writer. *Learning Difficulties Australia Bulletin, 51*(1), 17–21.

Cronbach, L. J. (1942). Measuring knowledge of precise word meaning. *The Journal of Educational Research, 36*(7), 528–534. https://doi.org/10.1080/00220671.1943.10881192

Cutler, L., & Graham, S. (2008). Primary grade writing instruction: A national survey. *Journal of Educational Psychology, 100*(4), 907–919. https://doi.org/10.1037/a0012656

Daffern, T., & Critten, S. (2019). Student and teacher perspectives on spelling. *Australian Journal of Language and Literacy, 42*(1), 40–57.

Dale, E., & O'Rourke, J. (1986). *Vocabulary building.* Zaner-Bloser.

Department for Education and Skills. (2007). *Letters and sounds: Principles and practice of high quality phonics.* https://assets.publishing.service.gov.uk/media/5a7aa7b6e5274a34770e630c/Letters_and_Sounds_-_DFES-00281-2007.pdf

Dockrell, J. E., Marshall, C. R., & Wyse, D. (2016). Teachers' reported practices for teaching writing in England. *Reading and Writing: An Interdisciplinary Journal, 29*(3), 409–434. https://doi.org/10.1007/s11145-015-9605-9

Duff, D., & Brydon, M. (2020). Estimates of individual differences in vocabulary size in English: How many words are needed to 'close the vocabulary gap'? *Journal of Research in Reading, 43*(4), 454–481. https://doi.org/10.1111/1467-9817.12322

Duke, N. K. (2000). 3.6 minutes per day: The scarcity of informational texts in first grade. *Reading Research Quarterly, 35*(2), 202–224. https://doi.org/10.1598/RRQ.35.2.1

Duke, N. K., Ward, A. E., & Pearson, P. D. (2021). The science of reading comprehension instruction. *The Reading Teacher, 74*(6), 663–672. https://doi.org/10.1002/trtr.1993

Dunn, D. M. D. (2018). *Peabody Picture Vocabulary Test – 5* (5th ed.). Pearson.

Durkin, D. (1978/79). What classroom observations reveal about reading comprehension instruction. *Reading Research Quarterly, 14*(4), 481–533. https://www.jstor.org/stable/747260

Dymock, S. (1993). Reading but not understanding. *Journal of Reading, 37*(2), 86–91.

Dymock, S. (2005). Teaching expository text structure awareness. *The Reading Teacher, 59*(2), 177–181. https://doi.org/10.1598/RT.59.2.7

Dymock, S. (2007). Comprehension strategy instruction: Teaching narrative text structure. *The Reading Teacher, 61,* 161–167.

Dymock, S. (2017). There must be a better way: The case against the New Zealand literacy strategy and some examples of how we can help students who fall by the wayside. *Literacy Forum NZ, 32*(3), 6–16.

Dymock, S. (2019). Yes, spelling should be taught. *Learning Difficulties Australia Bulletin, 51*(1), 22–24.

Dymock, S., & Nicholson, T. (2010). "High 5!" Strategies to enhance comprehension of expository text. *The Reading Teacher, 64*(3), 166–178. https://doi.org/10.1598/RT.64.3.2

Dymock, S., & Nicholson, T. (2012). *Teaching comprehension: The what, the why, and the how.* NZCER Press.

Dymock, S., & Nicholson, T. (2017). To what extent does spelling improve as a result of learning words with the look, say, cover, write, check, fix strategy compared with phonological spelling strategies? *Australian Journal of Learning Difficulties, 22*(2), 171–187.

Ehri, L. C., Nunes, S. R., Willows, D. M., Schuster, B. V., Yaghoub-Zadeh, Z., & Shanahan, T. (2001). Phonemic awareness instruction helps children learn to read: Evidence from the National Reading Panel's meta-analysis. *Reading Research Quarterly, 36*(3), 250–287. https://doi.org/10.1598/RRQ.36.3.2

Elleman, A. M., Lindo, E. J., Morphy, P., & Compton, D. L. (2009). The impact of vocabulary instruction on passage level comprehension of school-aged children: A meta-analysis. *Journal of Research on Educational Effectiveness, 2,* 1–44.

Esposito, R., Herbert, E., & Sumner, E. (2022). Capturing variations in how spelling is taught in primary school classrooms in England. *British Educational Research Journal, 49*, 70–92. https://doi.org/10.1002/berj.3829

Filderman, M. J., Austin, C. R., Boucher, A. N., O'Donnell, K., & Swanson, E. A. (2022). A meta-analysis of the effects of reading comprehension interventions on the reading comprehension outcomes of struggling readers in third through 12th grades. *Exceptional Children, 88*(2), 163–184. https://doi.org/10.1177/00144029211050860

Fox, M. (1983). *Possum magic*. Omnibus Books (or Scholastic).

Galuschka, K., Görgen, R., Kalmar, J., Haberstroh, S., Schmalz, X., & Schulte-Körne, G. (2020). Effectiveness of spelling interventions for learners with dyslexia: A meta-analysis and systematic review. *Educational Psychologist, 55*(1), 1–20. https:/doi.org/10.1080/00461520.2019.1659794

George, P. (2022a). *Markets*. Wendy Pye Publishing Ltd.

George, P. (2022b). *From here to there*. Wendy Pye Publishing Ltd.

Gough, P. B. (1983). Context, form, and interaction. In K. Rayner (Ed.), *Eye movements in reading* (pp. 203–211). Academic Press.

Gough, P. B. (1993). The beginning of decoding. *Reading and Writing, 5*, 181–192.

Gough, P. B. (1996). How children learn to read and why they fail. *Annals of Dyslexia, 46*, 3–20.

Gough, P. B., & Hillinger, M. L. (1980). Learning to read: An unnatural act. *Bulletin of the Orton Society, 30*, 179–196. https://doi.org/10.1007/BF02653717

Gough, P. B., & Lee, C. H. (2007). A step toward early phonemic awareness: The effects of turtle talk training. *Psychologia, 50*, 54–66.

Gough, P. B., & Tunmer, W. E. (1986). Decoding, reading, and reading disability. *RASE: Remedial and Special Education, 7(1)*, 6–10. https://doi.org/10.1177/074193258600700104

Gough, P. B., & Walsh, M. A. (1991). Chinese, Phoenicians, and the orthographic cipher of English. In S. A. Brady & D. P. Shankweiler (Eds.), *Phonological processes in literacy: A tribute to Isabelle I. Liberman* (pp. 199–209). Erlbaum.

Graham, S., Collins, A. A., & Rigby-Wills, H. (2017). Writing characteristics of students with learning disabilities and typically achieving peers: A meta-analysis. *Exceptional Children, 83(2)*, 199–218. https://doi.org/10.1177/0014402916664070

Graham, S., Harris, K. R., & Hebert, M. (2011). Is it more than just the message: Presentation effects in scoring writing. *Focus on Exceptional Children, 44*(4), 1–12. https://doi.org/10.17161/foec.v44i4.6687

Graham, S., McKeown, D., Kiuhara, S., & Harris, K. R. (2012). A meta-analysis of writing instruction for students in the elementary grades. *Journal of Educational Psychology, 104*(4), 879–896. https://doi.org/10.1037/a0029185

Graham, S., Morphy, P., Harris, K. R., Fink-Chorzempa, B., Saddler, B., Moran, S., & Mason, L. (2008). Teaching spelling in the primary grades: A national survey of instructional practices and adaptations. *American Educational Research Journal, 45*(3), 796–825. https://doi.org/10.3102/0002831208319722

Graham, S., & Santangelo, T. (2014). Does spelling instruction make students better spellers, readers, and writers? A meta-analytic review. *Reading and Writing: An Interdisciplinary Journal, 27*(9), 1703–1743. https://doi.org/10.1007/s11145-014-9517-0

Graves, M. F. (2006). *The vocabulary book: Learning and instruction*. Teachers College Press.

Graves, M. F., Juel, C., & Graves, B. B. (2004). *Teaching reading in the 21st century*. Pearson.

Harley, T. A. (2017). *Talking the talk: Language, psychology and science* (2nd ed.). Psychology Press.

Hart, B., & Risley, T. R. (1995). *Meaningful differences in the everyday experiences of young American children*. Paul H. Brookes Publishing.

Hart, B., & Risley, T. R. (2003). The early catastrophe: The 30 million word gap by age 3. *American Educator, 27*(1), 4–9.

Henry, M. (2010). *Unlocking literacy. Effective decoding and spelling instruction* (2nd ed.). Paul Brookes.

Hirsch, E. D. (2003). Reading comprehension requires knowledge – of words and the world. *American Educator, 27*(1), 10–13, 16–22, 28–29, 48.

Hirsch, E. D. Jr. (2006). *The knowledge deficit: Closing the shocking education gap for American children*. Houghton Mifflin.

Hirsch, E. D. (2016). *Why knowledge matters: Rescuing our children from failed educational theories*. Harvard Education Press. https://doi.org/10.1080/00071005.2017.1354531

Hjetland, H. N., Brinchmann, E. I., Scherer, R., & Melby-Lervåg, M. (2017). Preschool predictors of later reading comprehension ability: A systematic review. *Campbell Systematic Reviews, 14*, 1–155. https://doi.org/10.4073/csr.2017.14

Hjetland, H. N., Lervåg, A., Lyster, S. A., Hagtvet, B. E., Hulme, C., & Melby-Lervåg, M. (2019). Pathways to reading comprehension: A longitudinal study from 4 to 9 years of age. *Journal of Educational Psychology, 111*(5), 751–763. https://doi.org/10.1037/edu0000321

Hoover, W. A., & Gough, P. B. (1990). The simple view of reading. *Reading and Writing: An Interdisciplinary Journal, 2*(2), 127–160. https://doi.org/10.1007/BF00401799

Hoover, W. A., & Tunmer, W. E. (2020). *The cognitive foundations of reading and its acquisition*. Springer. https://doi.org/10.1080/03004279.2023.2173531

Hoover, W. A., & Tunmer, W. E. (2022). The primacy of science in communicating advances in the science of reading. *Reading Research Quarterly, 57*(2), 399–408.

Hresko, W. P., Herron, S. R., Peak, P. R., & Hicks, D. L. (2012). *Test of Early Written Language-3*. ProEd.

Hutchins, P. (1998) *Rosie's walk*. Bodley Head

Hwang, H., Cabell, S. Q., & Joyner, R. E. (2023). Does cultivating content knowledge during literacy instruction support vocabulary and comprehension in the elementary school years? A systematic review. *Reading Psychology, 44*(2), 145–174. https://doi.org/10.1080/02702711.2022.2141397

Iverson, S. (1995) *Farms*. Lands End.

James, K., & Berninger, V. (2019). Brain research shows why handwriting should be taught in the computer age. *Learning Difficulties Australia Bulletin, 51*(1), 25–30.

Johnson, D.D., Moe, A.J., & Baumann, J.F. (1983). *The Ginn word book for teachers: A basic lexicon*. Ginn.

Johnston, R., & Watson, J. (2004). Accelerating the development of reading, spelling, and phonemic awareness skills in initial readers. *Reading and Writing, 17*, 327–357.

Johnston, R. S., & Watson, J. E. (2005). *The effects of synthetic phonics teaching on reading and spelling attainment: A seven-year longitudinal study*. Scottish Executive Education Department.

Jorgenson, G. W. (1977). Relationship of classroom behavior to the accuracy of the match between material difficulty and student ability. *Journal of Educational Psychology, 69*(1), 24–32. https://doi.org/10.1037/0022-0663.69.1.24

Joseph, L. M., Alber-Morgan, S., Cullen, J., & Rouse, C. (2016). The effects of self-questioning on reading comprehension: A literature review. *Reading & Writing Quarterly, 32*(2), 152–173. https://doi.org/10.1080/10573569.2014.891449

Joshi, R. M., Treiman, R., Carreker, S., & Moats, L. (2008). How words cast their spell. Spelling is an integral part of learning the language, not a matter of memorization. *American Educator, 32*(4), 6–13, 16, 42.

Juel, C. (1988). Learning to reading and write: A longitudinal study of 54 children from first through fourth grades. *Journal of Educational Psychology, 80*, 437–447. https://doi.org/10.1037/0022-0663.80.4.437

Juel, C., Biancarosa, G., Coker, D., & Deffes, R. (2003). Walking with Rosie: A cautionary tale of early reading instruction. *Educational Leadership, 60*(7), 12–18.

Juel, C., Griffith, P. L., & Gough, P. B. (1986). Acquisition of literacy: A longitudinal study of children in first and second grade. *Journal of Educational Psychology, 78*(4), 243–255. https://doi.org/10.1037/0022-0663.78.4.243

Juel, C., & Minden-Cupp, C. (2003). One down and 80,000 to go: Word recognition instruction in the primary grades. *The Reading Teacher, 53*(4), 332–335.

Knowles, S. (1988). *Edward the Emu.* Harper Collins.

Kronholtz, J. (2010). Competition makes a comeback. Academic bees and bowls attract top students. *Education Next, 10*(3), 12–19.

Malpique, A. A., Valcan, D., Pino-Pasternak, D., & Ledger, S. (2023). Teaching writing in primary education (grades 1-6) in Australia: A national survey. *Reading and Writing, 36,* 119–145. https://doi.org/10.1007/s11145-022-10294-2

Mancilla-Martinez, J., & McClain, J. B. (2020). What do we know today about the complexity of vocabulary gaps and what do we not know? In E. B. Moje, P. P. Afflerbach, P. Enciso, & N. K. Lesaux (Eds.), *Handbook of reading research* (Vol. 5, pp. 216–236). Routledge. https://doi-org.ezproxy.massey.ac.nz/10.4324/9781315676302

Mandler, J. M., & Johnson, N. S. (1977). Remembrance of things parsed: Story structure and recall. *Cognitive Psychology, 9,* 111–151. https://doi.org/10.1016/0010-0285(77)90006-8

Mar, R. A., Li, J., Nguyen, A. T. P., & Ta, C. P. (2021). Memory and comprehension of narrative and expository texts: A meta-analysis. *Psychonomic Bulletin and Review, 28*(3), 732–749. https://doi.org/10.3758/s13423-020-01853-1

Marks, C. B., Doctorow, M. J., & Wittrock, M. C. (1974). Word frequency and reading comprehension. *The Journal of Educational Research, 67*(6), 259–262. https://doi.org/10.1080/00220671.1974.10884622

McKeown, M. G., Beck, I. L., Omanson, R. C., & Pople, M. T. (1985). Some effects of the nature and frequency of vocabulary instruction on the knowledge and use of words. *Reading Research Quarterly, 20*(5), 522–535. https://doi.org/10.2307/747940

McMaster, K. L., Kunkel, A., Shin, J., Jung, P.-G., & Lembke, E. (2018). Early writing intervention: A best evidence synthesis. *Journal of Learning Disabilities, 51*(4), 363–380. https://doi.org/10.1177/0022219417708169

McVee, M. B., Dunsmore, K., & Gavelek, J. R. (2005). Schema theory revisited. *Review of Educational Research, 75*(4), 531–566. https://doi.org/10.3102/00346543075004531

Meeks, L. J., & Kemp, C. R. (2017). How well prepared are Australian preservice teachers to teach early reading skills. *Australian Journal of Teacher Education, 42*(11), 1–17.

Meeks, L. J., & Stephenson, J. (2020). Australian preservice teachers and early reading instruction. *Australian Journal of Learning Difficulties, 25*(1), 65–82.

Merriam-Webster. (n.d.). Word. In Merriam-Webster.com dictionary. Retrieved April 20 2024, from https://www.merriam-webster.com/dictionary/word.

Miller, G. A. (1956). The magical number seven, plus or minus two: Some limits on our capacity for processing information. *Psychological Review, 63(2),* 81–97. https://doi.org/10.1037/h0043158

Nagy, W. (2005). Why vocabulary instruction needs to be long-term and comprehensive. In E. H. Hiebert & M. L. Kamil (Eds.), *Teaching and learning vocabulary: Bringing research to practice* (pp. 27–44). Lawrence Erlbaum.

Nagy, W. E., & Scott, J. A. (2000). Vocabulary processes. In M. L. Kamil, P. B. Mosenthal, P. D. Pearson, & R. Barr (Eds.), *Handbook of reading research* (Vol. 3, pp. 269–294). Lawrence Erlbaum.

Nation, P. (2020). The different aspects of vocabulary knowledge. In S. Webb (Ed.), *The Routledge handbook of vocabulary studies* (pp. 15–29). Routledge.

National Reading Panel (U.S.) & National Institute of Child Health and Human Development (U.S.). (2000). Report of the National Reading Panel: Teaching children to read: an evidence-based assessment of the scientific research literature on reading and its implications for reading instruction. U.S. Dept. of Health and Human Services, Public Health Service, National Institutes of Health, National Institute of Child Health and Human Development.

Nicholson, T. (1991). Do children read words better in context or in lists? A classic study revisited. *Journal of Educational Psychology*, *83*(4), 444–450. https://doi.org/10.1037/0022-0663.83.4.444

Nicholson, T. (2005). *Phonics handbook*. Wiley.

Nicholson, T., & Dymock, S. (2018). *Writing for impact. Teaching students how to write with a plan and spell well. (Vols. 1 and 2)*. NZCER Press.

Nicholson, T., & Dymock, S. (2023). *The New Zealand dyslexia handbook*. NZCER Press.

Nicholson, T., & Hill, D. (1985). Good readers don't guess – taking another look at the issue of whether children read words better in context or isolation. *Reading Psychology*, *6*(3–4), 181–198. https://doi.org/10.1080/0270271850060306

Nicholson, T., & McIntosh, S. (2020). An exploration of the relationship between phonological and phonics knowledge and self-efficacy for teaching. *Dyslexia*, *26*(3), 286–304. https://doi.org/10.1002/dys.1636

Nicholson, T., & Tunmer, W. E. (2010). Reading: The great debate. In C. Rubie-Davies (Ed.), *Educational psychology: Concepts, research, and challenges* (pp. 36–51). Routledge.

Nist, J. (1966). *A structural history of English*. St Martin's Press.

Okkinga, M., van Steensel, R. V., Gelderen, A. J., van Schooten, E., Sleegers, P. J., & Arends, L. R. (2018). Effectiveness of reading-strategy interventions in whole classrooms: A meta-analysis. *Educational Psychology Review*, *30*, 1215–1239. https://doi.org/10.1080/02702711.2021.1887019

O'Neill, S. (2016). Gradgrind Morgan is sucking the joy out of learning. *The Times*, p. 30.

Pan, S. C., Rickard, T. C., & Bjork, R. A. (2021). Does spelling still matter- and if so, how should it be taught? Perspectives from contemporary and historical research. *Educational Psychology Review*, *33*(4), 1523–1552. https://doi.org/10.1007/s10648-021-09611-y

Patrick, S. K. (2020). Homogeneous grouping in early elementary reading instruction: The challenge of identifying appropriate comparisons and examining differential associations between grouping and reading growth. *The Elementary School Journal*, *120*(4), 611–635. https://doi.org/10.1086/708666

Pearson, P. D., & Johnson, D. D. (1978). *Teaching reading comprehension*. Holt Rinehart Winston.

Pressley, M. (2000). What should comprehension instruction be the instruction of? In M. L. Kamil, P. B. Mosenthal, P. D. Pearson, & R. Barr (Eds.), *Handbook of reading research* (Vol. 3, pp. 545–561). Longman.

Pressley, M. (2008). What the future of reading research could be. In C. C. Block & S. R. Parris (Eds.), *Comprehension instruction: Research-based best practices* (pp. 391–413). Guilford Press.

Pressley, T., Allington, R. L., & Pressley, M. (2023). *Reading instruction that works: The case for balanced teaching* (5th ed.). Guilford Press.

Prochnow, J. E., Tunmer, W. E., & Chapman, J. W. (2013). A longitudinal investigation of the influence of literacy-related skills, reading self-perceptions, and inattentive behaviours on the development of literacy learning difficulties. *International Journal of Disability, Development, and Education*, *60*(3), 185–207.

Ralli, A. M., Kazali, E., Kanellou, M., Mouzaki, M., Antoniou, F., Diamanti, V., & Papaioannou, S. (2021). Oral language and story retelling during preschool and primary school years: Developmental patterns and interrelationships. *Journal of Psycholinguistic Research*, *50*, 949–965. https://doi.org/10.1007/s10936-021-09758-3

Rehfeld, D. M., Kirkpatrick, M., O'Guinn, N., Renbarger, R. (2022). A meta-analysis of phonemic awareness instruction provided to children suspected of having a reading disability. *Language, Speech, and Hearing Services in Schools*, *53*, 1177–1201. https://doi.org/10.1044/2022_LSHSS-21-00160

Rice, J. M. (1897). The futility of the spelling grind, I and II. *Forum*, *23*, 163–172 and 409–419.

Rice, M., Erbeli, F., Thompson, C. G., Sallese, M. R., & Fogarty, M. (2022). Phonemic awareness: A meta-analysis for planning effective instruction. *Reading Research Quarterly*, *57*(4), 1259–1289. https://doi.org/10.1002/rrq.473

Rippin, S. (2022). *Wild things: How we learn to read and what can happen if we don't.* Hardie Grant Children's Publishing.

Roper, H. D. (1984). *Spelling, word recognition and phonemic awareness among first grade students* [Unpublished doctoral dissertation, University of Texas, Austin, TX].

Rose, J. (2006) *Independent review of the early teaching of reading.* Department for Education and Skills. https://dera.ioe.ac.uk/5551/2/report.pdf

Rumelhart, D. (1980). Schemata: The building blocks of cognition. In R. Spiro, B. Bruce, & W. Brewer (Eds.), *Theoretical issues in reading comprehension* (pp. 33–58). Erlbaum.

Samson, D. (2015). Teaching punctuation. *The Virginia English Journal, 64*(2), 23–37.

Saragi, T., Nation, I. S. P., & Meister, G. F. (1978). Vocabulary learning and reading. *System, 6*(2), 72–78. https://doi.org/10.1016/0346-251X(78)90027-1

Schonell, F. J., & Schonell, F. E. (1956). *Diagnostic and attainment testing: Including a manual of tests, their nature, use, and interpretation* (3rd ed.). Oliver & Boyd.

Schultz, C. M. (2000). *Peanuts 2000: The 50th year of the world's favorite comic strip.* Ballantine.

Schulz, M. (2009). Effective writing assessment and instruction for young English language learners. *Early Childhood Education Journal, 37*, 57–62. https://doi.org/10.1007/s10643-009-0317-0

Scieszka, J. (1996). *The true story of the three little pigs.* Puffin.

Segbers, J., & Schroeder, S. (2017). How many words do children know? A corpus-based estimation of children's total vocabulary size. *Language Testing, 34*(3), 297–320.

Shanahan, T. (n.d.). *Improving reading comprehension in the primary classes.* National Council for Curriculum and Assessment. https://ncca.ie/media/4678/improving-reading-comprehension-in-the-primary-classes-professor-timothy-shanahan-university-of-illinois-at-chicago-1.pdf

Shanahan, T. (1984). Nature of the reading-writing relation: An exploratory multivariate analysis. *Journal of Educational Psychology, 76(3)*, 466–477. https://doi.org/10.1037/0022-0663.76.3.466

Sierra, J. (2010). *Tell the truth, B.B. Wolf.* Alfred A. Knopf.

Snow, C. (2002). *Reading for understanding: Toward a R and D program in reading comprehension.* RAND Corporation.

Stahl, K. A. D., Flanigan, K., & McKenna, M. C. (2019). *Assessment for reading instruction* (4th ed.). Guilford Press.

Stanback, M. L. (1992). Syllable and rime patterns for teaching reading: Analysis of a frequency-based vocabulary of 17,602 words. *Annals of Dyslexia, 42*, 196–221.

Stanovich, K. E. (1986). Matthew effects in reading: Some consequences of individual differences in the acquisition of literacy. *Reading Research Quarterly, 21*(4), 360–407.

Sternberg, R. J. (1987). Most vocabulary is learnt from context. In M. G. McKeown & M. Curtis (Eds.), *The nature of vocabulary acquisition* (pp. 89–105). Erlbaum.

Suggate, S. P. (2016). A meta-analysis of the long-term effects of phonemic awareness, phonics, fluency, and reading comprehension interventions. *Journal of Learning Disabilities, 49*(1), 77–96. https://doi.org/10.1177/0022219414528540

Thorndyke, P. W. (1977). Cognitive structures in comprehension and memory of narrative discourse. *Cognitive Psychology, 9*(1), 77–110. https://doi.org/10.1016/0010-0285(77)90005-6

Treiman, R. (2017). Learning to spell: Phonology and beyond. *Cognitive Neuropsychology, 34*(3–4), 83–93. https://doi.org/10.1080/02643294.2017.1337630

Tse, L., & Nicholson, T. (2014). The effect of phonics-enhanced Big Book reading on the language and literacy skills of 6-year-old pupils of different reading ability attending lower SES schools. *Frontiers in Psychology, 5*(1222). https://doi.org/10.3389/fpsyg.2014.01222

Trivizas, E. (2003). *The three little wolves and the big bad pig.* Egmont.

Wagner, J. (1977). *John Brown, Rose and the midnight cat.* Viking Kestrel.

Walker, D., Greenwood, C. R., Hart, B., & Carta, J. (1994). Prediction of school outcomes based on early language production and socioeconomic factors. *Child Development, 65*(2), 606–621. https://doi.org/10.2307/1131404

Wexler, N. (2019) *The knowledge gap: The hidden cause of America's broken education system – and how to fix it.* Avery.

White, E. B. (1963). *Charlotte's web.* Puffin.

Willingham, D. T. (2006–2007). The usefulness of brief instruction in comprehension strategies. *American Educator, 30*(4), 39–50.

Willingham, D. T. (2023–2024). Beyond comprehension. *Educational Leadership, 81*(4), 34–40.

Wyatt-Smith, C., Jackson, C., Boooah, V., & Whalley, K. (2018). *Summary of the research report of the Australian writing survey.* Institute for Learning Sciences and Teacher Education, Australian Catholic University.

Yeung, P., Ho, C. S., Chan, D. W., & Chung, K. K. (2017). The role of transcription skills and oral language in Chinese writing among children in upper elementary grades. *Applied Psycholinguistics, 38*(1), 211–231. http://dx.doi.org/10.1017/S0142716416000163

Zinsser, W. (2006). *On writing well.* Harper Collins.

Author index

Topic index

Note: Page numbers in bold denote tables, page numbers in italics denote figures.

For Product Safety Concerns and Information please contact our EU
representative GPSR@taylorandfrancis.com Taylor & Francis Verlag GmbH,
Kaufingerstraße 24, 80331 München, Germany

Printed and bound by CPI Group (UK) Ltd, Croydon, CR0 4YY
08/06/2025
01897005-0013